OUR SPIRITUAL JOURNEY

A Dreamstairway Book

OUR SPIRITUAL JOURNEY

———

THE LANGUAGE OF LIFE

by

CHARLES MILTON SMITH

ISBN 978-1-907091-02-5

British Library Cataloguing in Publication Data
A catalogue record for this book is available from the British Library

Published in the UK by Dreamstairway
© Dreamstairway 2009

www.dreamstairway.co.uk

FOREWORD

CHARLES MILTON SMITH is a historian and symbologist. For the past few decades he has been following the spiritual path of *Susila Budhi Dharma* (normally shortened to the acronym Subud), which is a means of orientating the individual towards spiritual reality – the truth that underlies and overlays the whole of life. It brings about the understanding that not only every individual, but the whole human race in historical terms is obliged to take a quite involuntary journey away from their high spiritual origins (the pure integrity of the newborn child, and the mythological Garden of Eden). This journey takes them through the minefield of instinctual 'passions' that fill the world of nature, until, reaching maturity, they become filled with the 'instincts' of materiality.

This book describes the great spiritual descent in terms of mythology, for myths have always constituted our ancestors' intuitive way of characterising these things. We have journeyed all the way from Eden to the very gates of Hades, and the time has come for us to begin the return journey. This is where Subud comes in, for the means of taking this return journey is the meaning and purpose of *Susila Budhi Dharma*. Whatever your religion, or even if you have no religious allegiance whatsoever, it should make little difference. If you find that some of the words or descriptions in this book offend you, simply change them, and use your own words, your own terms of reference. Words are no more than just words; religions are full of conflicting words, and religious beliefs, mere symbols of spiritual reality, are a matter of importance more for the mortal heart than for the immortal soul.

CONTENTS

Introduction   page 9

1   The Vibrations of Nature   page 11

Seeing through the materiality of the world to discover the intangible spirits of nature, which we can recognise as the driving instincts of animals, plants, and minerals. Together they form a pervasive network of vibrations or passions which are all too readily imbibed by the human psyche. How material advancement through the ages has corresponded with a decline in spiritual status.

2   Dawn Awakening   page 24

The earliest thinking reactions to natural phenomena: dawn, the sun, the moon, the weather. Clinging to the concept of a father figure by visualising a symbolic heavenly hierarchy to explain natural laws. The planets considered as symbols of the human condition.

3   Ripples of Emotion   page 40

Lakes, rivers, waterfalls, fountains, the sea; most people like to be near moving water, which seems to enhance their emotional expression. Whatever mood an emotional person brings to the waterside tends to be intensified and broadened to include non-personal elements.

4   Deep Waters of Spirit   page 61

Water may be taken to symbolise spirit: something that cannot be grasped or even explained in material terms, something from beyond our range of emotions, and unfathomable by the mind. Holy water, the sacred rivers of the East, these are the tangible symbols of intangible spirit.

CONTENTS

5   Beasts and Birds   page 72

The world of wildlife with its varied instincts comprised the first spiritual temptation for early mankind seeking to expand their opportunities. Through their own basic human instincts our ancestors acquired a vast complex of alien instincts, and these are still with us today.

6   Insect Dharma   page 90

The amazing world of Beelzebub, Lord of the Flies. The instinctive vibrations of the insect world are close to the surface, the most tangible and the most invasive. We need to appreciate the beauty and ingenuity of insects whilst avoiding their malign influence.

7   The Plant Kingdom   page 103

The unsuspected potency of the plant kingdom at the level of instinct: seemingly peaceful and submissive, in spirit aggressive and confrontational. How humans can avoid imbibing these fierce passions by allowing plants to find their own peaceful level.

8   The Cycle of Nature   page 127

The endless cycle of birth, life and death has occupied the minds of thinking people for thousands of years, affecting lives and livelihoods, and inspiring hope for some sort of life after death. Belief in human reincarnation has been prompted by awareness of this essential natural cycle.

9   Forest and Mountain   page 147

There is a narrow boundary between the cultivated and the untamed. The clearing between forest and farm is a point of destruction leading to new creation, and the place where woodland spirits congregate. Wild places produce a sense of awe by their grandeur.

10   Subtle Materiality   page 163

Crystals, ley lines, sacred sites, relics, bombs and guns: all are manifestations of the spiritual nature of the material life force, formed by way of the natural instincts of things. There is far more to this powerful force than meets the eye.

11   The Goddess Within   page 177

The laws of nature have resulted in the less-than-desirable spiritual level of humankind today. Spiritual laws are not to be assuaged by masculine aggressive confrontation. They may however be swayed by the feminine properties of intercession and submission.

12   Transcending Nature   page 186

The great dream of Gaia is to awaken to the perfection of the human psyche, and this can be done only by following the cycle of nature and the process of evolution on the inner level. Spiritual vibrations can stir the inner self and set the soul on its ultimate quest.

Index   page 198

We have all travelled from the spiritual to the material. It is now time for us to make the return journey, from the material back to the spiritual again.

Muhammad Subuh

INTRODUCTION

IN ANCIENT TIMES, people were aware of the spiritual dimension of nature, and felt themselves to be a part of this spirituality in a way quite unknown to most people today. The solid materiality of the world and all its creations was no doubt as self-evident then as it is now, but at that time it had far less effect on the human psyche than is the case today. We have heard of the vibrations of nature, which some people call the natural life forces: these forces are made up of all the instincts, the automatic actions and reactions that keep nature on course and give life to the planet. There are human instincts or life forces, animal life forces, plant life forces, and around and within all the rest, giving them form and substance and strength, the material life forces: the instincts that compel atoms to combine in certain ways and keep the universe functioning.

All the wealth, the comforts, the treasures, the technology of the world is to be found, not in the plant world, nor in the animal world, nor even in the purely human world, but within the material zone: and this broad field of material instincts proves an irresistible attraction for humankind; it is the provider of substantial wherewithal, and the home of civilisation. At the outset, when people were purely 'human'. they were comparatively helpless, naked creatures who lived in the world of instinct – the original 'Garden of Eden'. Below them in spiritual status were the life forces of nature, which, looked at as a whole, possessed an infinitely broader range of instinctive solutions to life's problems than that which could apply to humans alone. The Garden of Eden is not for thinkers. As the human brain developed and passions grew, those early humans became more and more engrossed in the vibrations, or the instinctual solutions, of the natural world beneath them. And as they acquired the skill to make and use artefacts, the material life forces (which already possessed their bodies) gradually took over their souls too.

OUR SPIRITUAL JOURNEY

An instinctive awareness of this spiritual descent gave rise to the stories of mythology which have been handed down to us. Stories which are merely products of the imagination tend not to be remembered and handed down; but ancient myths to explain the spiritual descent of humans, even after thousands of years, still have a place in our hearts, though they may not be completely understood by our minds. We are instinctively aware of their importance, and modern fiction, however clever, lacks their meaningful content. When natural spiritual decline passes a certain milestone myths can no longer be created, because spirituality itself is no longer a source of inspiration: no longer part of our normal awareness. In mythological terms we have all trodden a downhill route from Eden to the gates of Hades itself, and the time has come to seek for ourselves that path, that way, that return journey that will take us back to the very gates of heaven. That journey is *upwards* and away from materiality, *upwards* through the plant life forces, the animal life forces, the human life forces, to regain the point of human entry — the place of rebirth and the life beyond.

CHAPTER ONE

The Vibrations of Nature

NATURE IS FULL of unseen life forces: the spirits of nature. It doesn't matter whether you believe in the supernatural or not; belief doesn't really come into it. It is enough simply to be aware of this unseen dimension, to understand the principle of it. It comprises the spark of life common to all and based on natural laws.

For a start we need to stand back and take a broadly based overall view of the world of nature. We will see solid materiality wherever we look – rocks, soil, water, trees, flowers, beasts and birds and bees. But if we stand still further back and take a still broader view, we may begin to appreciate that everything we see (or don't see) runs on natural laws, powered by an invisible but highly complex network of vibrations; of compelling instincts.

The world of nature runs on instincts, on natural laws applicable to every life form: to every level of being, both animate and inanimate, material and abstract. Take the animals for instance: instinct alone provides the driving power to ensure that the 'king of the beasts' behaves and feeds like a lion, like all the other lions on the African plain; it provides the essential drive to ensure that the king's dinner, an antelope perhaps, behaves and feeds like all the other antelopes of its kind. These creatures do not have to reason and ponder over what they have to do, what they have to eat, where they have to live: they just go ahead and do it. Plainly these instincts are themselves unlearnt and unreasoned, yet they are only a small part of an incredibly complex and finely worked-out overall plan.

Unlike plants, animals are not rooted to the ground, and are therefore free to roam. But although on the face of it they may seem as free as the air they breathe, we can appreciate that they are quite unable to venture beyond their own allotted limits. They are wholly controlled by their instincts, and these controlling instincts are the outward and visible signs of what we might call the spiritual life forces of the earth, governing all its creatures. The life forces that show themselves by way of the appropriate set of instincts to guide each species are truly the gods and goddesses of all wild nature.

Animal life forces direct the lifestyle of the giant blue whale, guiding its movements through the world's oceans and inspiring it to sing its own beautiful song of life. Just as surely these unseen forces direct the lifestyle and movements of the tiniest microbes, and perhaps they too have their own beautiful songs. The spiritual life forces of animals are responsible for maintaining the strict social orders in the teeming world of insects, with their million-fold varieties of lifestyle. The same forces are responsible for the amazing migrations of birds, as well as salmon and eels.

Instinctual life forces are the root source of energy and strength, responsible for the positive joys of life as well as the negative results of arrogance and selfishness. This contradiction means that the creatures beneath their sway are fated to experience both ups and downs, the joys of triumph and new life, and the sorrows of defeat and ultimate death. Instincts lead the hounds to outrun the fox, and equally lead the fox to outwit the hounds. Instincts, it seems, are constantly in a state of tension within themselves, but they are at one with the earth. In essence, animal instincts are good and beneficial to the earth, for they ensure an even balance of populations and resources.

Plants function on their own individual brand of instinct to an even greater extent than animals do: they are completely bound by them, and this is their spiritual nature. No plant can think its way through life from the germination of its seed to its final extinction in the forest mould. The plant life forces bestow the instinctive urge to behave, as it may be, in the one like an oak tree, in another like a nettle, or a cactus, or a vine. Plant instincts, like those of the animals, are also good, for they create the natural balance upon which all other creatures depend.

At first glance, plants themselves may seem easy-going, serene, peace-loving creations. But on further consideration we can see that they are nothing of the sort: they are in a state of tension with each other. Plants, of course, are bound to the earth by their roots. Pollen and some types of seed are wind-borne, but apart from primitive plant forms and algae which drift in the ocean currents, they cannot move from their place of birth to look for a better place to live. As often as not it is their fate to have to struggle in the most hostile of environments. In making the best of what they have, plants must be ruthlessly competitive if they are to survive beyond the seedling stage. Their own instincts push them into battle. If they cannot adapt themselves to the competition of nearby plants, they have no option but to fight to the death in a constant struggle for light, food and moisture.

Animals usually have a sense of family, or group, or species. They feed their young, and may look after their own in various ways. To this extent at least they are not completely selfish. But with plants there is no such consideration. The welfare of neighbouring plants – even siblings from the same pod, or twins cloned from the same branch – is of no concern to them. Their rule in life is 'look after number one!'

An ancient forest may seem the most peaceful of places, but in spiritual terms it certainly is not. These fierce and selfish plant instincts will have been working to balance themselves out over many generations, so that their ceaseless strife has led to the formation of a closely-knit plant community. A wild community such as a forest is able to function as a unit only by virtue of inter-relating instincts: roots grow each at their own optimum depth so that every tree can draw its necessary food and moisture; each leaf must find enough sunlight to effect photosynthesis, so the foliage of each species is programmed to spread at differing heights and distinctive patterns in order to achieve this end.

The sex life of plants is highly imaginative — it has to be, for living creatures such as these which are immobile and rooted to the ground. Although many plants have both male and female flowers, self-pollination is the equivalent of inbreeding, and must be avoided if possible. Sometimes the wind serves to scatter pollen in the hope of a few grains landing where they are needed. In other cases insects are induced to visit the flowers for food, and in so doing carry the fertilising pollen from flower to flower. There are even flowers which look like the females of certain insects, so as to entice any randy males around and to manoeuvre them into the best position to coat their backs with pollen, or to brush the pollen they already carry against the receptive female parts of the flower. Each plant has its own individually designed method of ensuring reproduction, dispersal of the resultant seeds, and subsequent survival of the species. It would be hard to believe that there is no comprehensive and very imaginative intelligence behind all this.

Even within an apparently peaceful plant community, each plant remains wholly individual. If that peaceful community is disturbed by whatever cause, it is a case of every plant for itself. Should one plant find itself temporarily at an advantage, it wastes no time in taking over as much territory as it can, suppressing any other plants in the process. A peaceful woodland community evolves only through this instinctive passion of ruthless selfishness, each plant co-existing apparently in harmony, but always in a state of readiness to take advantage of any signs of weakness.

Finally, below the plants, there is solid ground. The material life forces can be said to project the impulse, to form the instincts dictating the behaviour of atoms and all the particles that make up the body of the earth, regulating the form and density of solids, liquids, and gases, of minerals and metals, soil and rocks. And of course plants, animals and humans are all material objects too — at least as far as the cells of their bodies, their outward forms, are concerned. Even our thoughts are the product of our material brains. The material instincts are perhaps the least subtle of all these nebulous life forces. They are certainly the coarsest, the heaviest, the most tangible, and ultimately the most powerful. We can see that the world could not possibly exist without them. They constitute the mechanics of gravity and magnetism, controlling the tendency of matter to accumulate or disperse. Sound waves, radio waves, force fields, ley lines, even the mysterious properties of crystals, all these represent the concentrated workings of the material life force.

Look at these life forces, these instinctive vibrations, from man's viewpoint: they can be visualised as four distinct layers of passion, of driving energy, each separated by an invisible but very real barrier, and these barriers work something like a one-way valve. As though playing a giant board game called life, human beings start as children in the topmost layer. It is comparatively easy for them to descend, progressively acquiring new layers of instinct, of passion, until they reach the material core. This is the general state of affairs both in an individual lifetime and in the history of humankind. But it is far more difficult for an adult human, once having sunk, as it were, to rock bottom, to climb back if he or she feels the need to sample again the truly human life force.

Primitive mankind was driven by what we might call the human instinct – that is, the human life force undiluted or unadulterated by thoughtful desires and innocent of civilisation. This is, or was, the simple state which the story of Genesis in the Bible calls the 'Garden of Eden', a peaceful place of hunters and gatherers. People then, no doubt, were excellent observers; but they were not thinkers. As soon as people began to think for themselves and to desire more than the bare necessities of life, they began to sink into the level of the animal life forces, which they imbibed as well as their own human instincts. The Bible again calls this the 'temptation of the serpent'. Other mythical accounts of human life long ago have described the fabled guardian of the animal level and the other spiritual levels below it, as Cerberus, the three-headed dog which guards the underworld and welcomes people into its domain, but prevents them leaving. Other stories have described dragons which guard the earth's treasures, or a gigantic bird called the roc (a word which originally meant a spiritual force capable of transporting human souls), The Arabian Nights story of Sindbad the Sailor tells how a roc carried him over the mountains and deposited him in a deep valley strewn with jewels – a telling description of the rewards and perils represented by the material life force.

When primitive humans stopped being hunters and gatherers and began to rear and tend flocks, they were at first nomads, ranging over the land and pitching their tents wherever the grazing seemed best. Finally they saw the wisdom of settling down in one place, and established farms and villages, cultivating the soil and growing crops as well as rearing farm animals. The territorial instincts of animals have a powerful effect upon the humans who fall under their spell, and they are the inspiration for the ownership of land and the formation of personal and national boundaries. Previously it was the land, in effect, that owned the people. Now the people felt obliged to own their own piece of land, and this sense of ownership led to a degree of animal-style diplomacy, often sealing borders with a threatening display of force held at the ready, always jostling for space.

For many centuries mankind lived, as it were, within the maw of the animal life force, not realising of course that their whole lifestyle, attitudes, values, and even their religions, were based on the lives of the beasts around them. Such people often thought it a good idea to slaughter some of their beasts as a religious sacrifice, and wealthy people vied with each other to see who could sacrifice the most. The biblical king Solomon broke all records in the 10th century BC when he sacrificed 120,000 sheep and 22,000 oxen at one session. Human populations were increasing, and all the time they were steadily cutting down forests, clearing new farm land. They began to be ever more jealously possessive over land use, and friction between groups grew until they met a new monster to take over their lives: the Green Man.

THE VIBRATIONS OF NATURE

Like the plants upon which they and their herds depended, people unwittingly under the sway of the Green Man – a personification of the spiritual plant life force – came to be more aggressive than previously in their possession of land. They saw nothing wrong in taking someone else's land by force if they could get away with it. They grew less tolerant, quicker to blame and to punish. It was a time of superstition and cruelty, and religions too became more unforgiving. Other races were seldom tolerated. Quarrels and smouldering jealousies over land ownership often developed into out and out warfare.

Slavery, which had begun during the old animal life force days, grew apace, and the treatment of slaves became even less humane. In the past people had been treated as though they were animals; now people tended to treat each other as though they were plants, disposing of them as if they were chopping and burning unwanted vegetation. When the Romans invaded Celtic lands they reported that the natives built giant 'green men' made of wood, branches and wickerwork, covered with sprigs of green foliage, and into these huge effigies live animals and humans were thrown before being burnt alive. Even the cruel Romans were shocked, for their own brand of cruelty in the arenas, like their empire-building, was based upon the animal rather than the plant life forces.

After the horrors of the Green Man, the 'rule of Satan' came as something of a relief for mankind. Satan, or the *roc satani*, is merely an ancient name for the material life force, the supernatural power that oversees the functioning of materiality. Because this material force stands opposed to the non-material essence of spirituality, and holds so great an attraction for people, inevitably Satan has become identified with the force of evil opposed to the goodness of God. But as described in the biblical book of Job, Satan was originally thought of as a 'son of God', a member of the court of heaven, whose function it was to 'range over the earth'. We are all closely acquainted with the workings of the material life forces, for they form the basis of our civilisation with all its trappings. If you wish to know what a 'satanic' person looks like, look all around you: look in the mirror!

These overwhelming life forces and the way they have affected humans over the ages by way of the natural 'instincts' of material and apparently lifeless things, as well as living plants and animals, are summarised in the table on page 20. Once these natural qualities have been pointed out, I suppose they are fairly obvious; but they are certainly not the sort of thing most modern people think about. Nevertheless we could do worse than to bear them in mind if we want to understand these elemental spirits of nature, to tune into their vibrations; to make best use of them, and finally to leave them behind.

Primitive humans were at the top of their particular tree. They knew the ways of the animals they hunted, the characteristics of the plants they made use of. They were probably not, at that stage, too concerned with 'gods and goddesses' – they were 'all of a piece' and saw the world more or less as a whole: they were still in a state of spiritual wholeness, and the 'Father Figure' was their symbolic ruler. It was only when people began to leave behind the innocent state of Eden and sink, as it were, to the level of animals – in practice, to acquire animal instincts for themselves – and actually to make use of their brain-power, their thoughts and emotions, that their wholeness began to fragment, and inevitably with the development of imagination they became increasingly superstitious about their world.

These early humans began to suspect, too, that some animals seemed to possess a higher spiritual level than their own, and it was true: their human spiritual status had diminished to that extent. It was a time in early human history when totem animals came to be recognised. Practical totemism is still to be found among tribal peoples in America, Africa, Asia, and Australia, and it happens when the spiritual awareness of some particular creature impinges so strongly on the human awareness that a special relationship with it is developed. Later, as spiritual fragmentation increased and people descended still further on the spiritual ladder of life, plants too started to become the totem objects of clanship. Nowadays numerous material icons no doubt play their role.

THE VIBRATIONS OF NATURE

Of course, things did not stop there. All through prehistory and history people have been sinking lower in spiritual terms, leaving the human life force behind as they passed through the animal, then the plant, finally to enter the material life force. And as this process was happening, everybody was becoming more and more civilised, human brains were becoming more and more astute, feelings more and more sensitive, the sense of desire and the need for possessions more and more powerful.

It was during this great descent that the spirits of nature began to take shape in the minds of men and grow in strength and individuality. Ghosts, elves, nymphs, goddesses and gods of the forest became more real than the symbolic Father Figure of Eden. A multitude of variations on the masculine theme of Pan, and the feminine theme of Diana, took on greater and greater importance. In ancient Babylon, for instance, the common people recognised some four thousand gods and goddesses, besides innumerable demons and goblins to keep them company. We can now see that these were not merely figments of the superstitious imagination: they were and still are the living forces that connect spirituality with materiality. Their presence, each with its own brand of consciousness, could actually be felt by the people whose simple lives were dominated by the animal and the plant life forces.

The material life force is dense and powerful enough to block out these feelings. When the material level has been reached by the human psyche, awareness of them all but disappears. Science – discovering how things work, how the universe functions in material terms and the best ways for us to manipulate it – tends to despise anything that cannot be seen, or measured, or proved. This is why people with exceptionally clever brains often find it difficult or impossible to comprehend the notion of an Almighty God, the epitome of wholeness itself, because such people feel the need to analyse, and analysis destroys wholeness. Their personal fragmentation has been healed, but in the material sense only. Their brand of wholeness, the integrity of *things*, acts like a cloak that shuts out the light.

Life force	Symbolic ruler	Lifestyle
HUMAN	The Father Figure	Hunter-gatherers: desire for individuality and personal ownership rather than tribal allegiance led their descent from the instinctive state symbolised by the garden of Eden
ANIMAL	The Serpent	Nomadic grazers: forming relations with other groups, creating racial boundaries. Territorial wrangling leading to diplomacy and a wish for permanent settlement
PLANT	The Green Man	Agriculturists: increasingly selfish possession of land and resources leading to competitiveness, defensiveness, intolerance, ethnic aggression and warfare
MATERIAL	Satan	Industrialists: present-day Western society able to make best use of natural resources. Science and mechanisation leading to increasing desire for national and personal wealth and power

The challenge now is to reverse the process; having travelled as it were from the spiritual to the material, having understood how everything works, we should now be able to travel back to the spiritual source, carrying all that we need for our welfare with us. It is our destiny that we should possess an even blend of all these life forces, enabling us to become well-balanced people. In the process we can make best use of these varied instincts while releasing ourselves from their spell.

Please don't think of all this as yet another theory, or some sort of religious notion. It is real: we have imbibed these subtle influences during our own lives and by way of our ancestors, until they are part of us. Some people seek to 'commune' with the spirits of nature, and they really can do this, in a way that is probably beyond their own expectations. But if someone calls upon such and such a spirit and receives a response, you may discover that they are actually calling upon and contacting something that is already a small part of themselves. If we 'tune in' to some aspect of nature, we will be tuning in to a previously unnoticed part of ourselves. If we think we are conversing with demons, we may discover that we have actually been talking to ourselves. If we believe ourselves to be conversing with saints – why, once again a dormant part of our own selves has been aroused and may well respond. The inner self, we can say, is vastly larger than the outer self, with the capacity to expand without limit.

The Vibration of the Inner Self

If a religious man calls upon God, and receives an answer to his prayers, he will have received that result only because he has been praying successfully to the highest part of himself. This is not to deny the reality of God the creator. God the impersonal may be the ultimate reality, but he can only be known or apprehended in the form of God the personal. A person may know the Holy Spirit only if that impersonal spirit first quickens and enters his or her personal soul, and this awakened soul is what he or she will come to know.

Pious people will sooner or later come to understand that the laws, rules, principles and powers of the religion that they follow – even if they are convinced that theirs is the only true religion – are but the symbols of spiritual reality, and not that reality itself. Spirit is abstract and above nature; religion is material and contained within nature. Mortal man cannot be expected to encompass spiritual reality. What *is* knowable is the self, and only the contents of the self, whatever has entered into that self, whether high or low, can be known. And at the final judgment only the quickened soul can stand in judgment of the actions and contents of the heart. The same is true of any culture and any religion, however cloaked in words and beliefs. This, surely, is the beginning of spiritual fulfilment: the experience of getting in touch with the deeper, the higher, the broader, the immortal part of your own self.

A very young child knows its own true self, though unable to express it in words. Any memory of this early knowledge soon becomes blocked out by the evolving brain with its thoughts, feelings and worldly influences; but this artless wisdom of babyhood is truly a treasure to be regained. The child learns its appropriate human language quite naturally by hearing it spoken; and in parallel with the evolution of the entire human race, the process of growing up involves the unconscious absorption of the vibrations that are all around us: the instinctual, multiple tongues of nature. This complex set of languages or influences completes the process of carrying us down to earth, in the spiritual sense. Our own long-concealed human nature, once reawakened, enables us to grasp what has happened and seek to make amends. The inherent process of learning by rote has produced civilisation with all its benefits; understanding and interpreting these instinctual languages calls for a spiritual orientation – a facing away from the materiality which is all around us, and inwards towards the self. This is the non-material direction of prayer.

There is really no further need to *learn* the languages of nature; quite unconsciously we have already done that. What we now need is to understand them, and learn to place them on a conscious level so that they are no longer merely instinctive, no longer a matter of fate. We need to find a way to set our thinking and our emotional feeling on one side, if only temporarily, while still fully conscious. If we are able to do this, we will experience the vibration of our own inner self – the truly human vibration that gives movement to a newborn child. Our psychic orientation will not then be set towards acquiring more, bigger and better *things*, for unlike a newborn baby we have already acquired all the materiality we need. Rather, it will be set towards a letting-go of the desire for these things, releasing what has become an addiction for us, initiating a movement away from our material base, setting the soul on a spiritual journey. Our odyssey will take us through the realm of plants, through the kingdom of animals, through the original level of human instinct, until we finally reach the point of birth, the place of original wisdom. Now, however, it will be our point of rebirth, and this in turn will open up the way to a continuing and possibly unlimited adventure of the soul.

Chapter Two

Dawn Awakening

SHE WAS DESCRIBED in ancient literature as a beautiful maiden with rosy-red fingers, her arms shading through shell pink to the pure white of her shapely shoulders and spreading wings, their flight feathers tipped with gleaming gold. Her hair was flaming auburn, her robe and mantle saffron, darkening at the hem. To announce the arrival of her father, the sun god, she would leave her mother, the goddess of night, and rise over the eastern horizon, dripping dew from a gold and silver vase, before riding away across the sea in a golden chariot drawn by white horses.

She was of course Aurora, the Roman goddess of dawn, known to the Greeks as Eos. A primeval archetype from the collective unconscious, in taking her place in the conscious imagination of men, perhaps she represented the first dawning of sentimentality being applied to the daily phenomena of nature. In the dawn, after all, there was nothing to fear, nothing to appease. Admiration was all that was needed. Before Aurora the heavens were less beautiful, less accommodating, and less friendly. People were grimly aware of the discomfort arbitrarily inflicted upon them by the elements, the wet, the cold, the scorching heat; and even when conditions seemed ideal, there still loomed the constant threat of possible horrors in store at the hands of unapproachable but all-seeing gods who dwelt in the sky.

How did our ancestors view their world? which of their experiences clung deeply enough to form the building blocks of new societies, new enterprises? Ancient writings give us some idea, and we can well appreciate how the intuitively creative stories of mythology attempted to explain the inexplicable, the spiritual content of everyday reality, while at the same time playing so large a part in assembling that vast store of images held within the collective unconscious. We might find what we are looking for by following the steps of human descent, and having done so, to reverse as it were the process of evolution and retrace our steps in a way that will recapture the old sense of wonder without sacrificing our own modern knowledge. By so doing we might even rediscover our own Garden of Eden.

When spiritual fragmentation had taken place; when people had left the truly human level of spirituality behind, lost touch with their 'Father Figure' and become immersed in the instinctual level more appropriate to animals, and being as yet unfamiliar with the trappings of materiality as we know them, there was a general tendency to look for objects of worship. Ancient historical records confirm that people in general needed to be shielded from 'images', from artefacts or carvings representing people or natural objects, lest they be driven to worship them. Nowadays there are so many images or 'carvings' on all sides that an attitude of superstitious reverence towards them might seem ridiculous − but we can identify vestiges of this situation in some religious cultures even today. Easier to understand perhaps is the viewing of natural phenomena, the sun and moon and all the 'hosts of heaven', as manifestations of divine power and worthy of reverence.

At the very beginning of that long, slippery descent from the Garden of Eden, probably, the sun was worshipped as a god, and this is understandable. There is no more godlike phenomenon that daily impinges on our lives. In the 13th century BC when Moses was leading his people on their forty-year nomadic journey through the desert wilderness, he found it necessary to warn them:

Take ye therefore good heed ... lest thou lift up thine eyes unto heaven, and when thou seest the sun, and the moon, and the stars, even all the hosts of heaven, shouldest thou be driven to worship them, which the Lord thy God hath divided unto all the nations under the whole heaven.

We can conclude from this that his chief objection was based on the fact that the heavenly host had been provided for all, rather than merely for the chosen people, to whom exclusivity was all-important. In retrospect it is readily seen that Moses was leading his Bronze Age tribesmen through what we have called the realm of the Serpent (he actually bore a bronze serpent on a pole as a standard), through the 'animal' instinctual level, in contrast with their truly human ancestors who had lived, we can surmise, in the time of Abraham many centuries earlier.

Elsewhere throughout the Middle Eastern lands the sun, worshipped wholeheartedly, had many qualities and many names. He was variously known by ancient Greeks, Romans and Sabians as Apollo, Helios, Phoebus, and Lycius. He was usually considered to have been the twin brother of Selene or Artemis in her role as the moon, and the father of Aurora or Eos, the dawn. Like his beautiful daughter he too rode a golden chariot drawn by four snowy-white horses. In his journeys across the heavens he has been called Phaeton, the brilliant one, and Panoptes, the all-seer. In ancient Babylon and Assyria he was the god Shamash. The Phoenicians and Syrians called him Heliogabalus, the bringer of light. He was Mithras, the Persian god of light, and in the northern parts of Assyria he was Asshur, or Nisroch – the god mentioned in the Bible at a time, during the 8th century BC, when the sun was apparently playing strange tricks. As a sign to the prophet Isaiah, the shadow on the sundial of Ahaz was said to have moved backwards by 10 degrees, a reflection perhaps of its strange behaviour at the time of Joshua's battles some 500 years earlier.

With all his names, he was first and foremost the Golden Apollo – or as Shakespeare put it, the 'fire-rob'd god'. Without the sun, of course, there could be no plants, no animals, no people, no nature, no life. This plain fact underlines Apollo's important status in mythology. Inevitably, he was the god of all crops, their maturing and ripening, particularly perhaps of fruit. He was able to protect crops against pests, from mildew and fungal infections, from the nibbling of mice and the devastations of locusts. Apollo too was divine patron of animal husbandry, of herds, flocks and pastures, and shepherds especially called upon him to protect their sheep from attacks by wolves. But Apollo had his bad side too: he was the overlord of illness, of infectious diseases, able to scatter deadly plagues over the earth, or eradicate them as he chose. He was a god to be feared as well as adored, able to punish and reward. It was in Apollo's power to cause despair among those who depended on the success of their crops and the welfare of their beasts. Various ceremonies were universally devised in the hope of pleasing Apollo and dissuading him from wreaking havoc.

Within temperate climatic zones, the seasons seem to accentuate the power of the sun to control the cycle of nature. To ensure the safe ripening of their crops, European farmers would hold spring festivals in honour of 'the approaching god'. Later in the year when leaves and buds became scorched by the summer sun, midsummer festivals of Apollo were held to beg his forbearance; and towards autumn when crops were ripening, the time of year when dry sunny weather was needed most urgently, further festivals were held. As autumn arrived and the crops were brought in, harvest festivals were devised in honour of 'the departing god'. Harvest festivals are happy occasions everywhere in rural communities. Peasant farmers offered the first fruits of autumn; sprigs of olive and bay were bunched with tassels of coloured wool and carried in procession along with baskets of fruit and vegetables, berries, olive oil, wine, honey and cakes. Householders would play their part, hanging evergreen branches over their doors and windows as the processions passed by.

Attributes of the Sun

During the second half of the 20th century AD it became very fashionable to sunbathe, to the extent that many people could be said to worship Apollo with renewed intensity. Earlier in the century, and during the whole of the 19th century AD, few northern Europeans would have considered baring their bodies to the sun's rays. It was simply not done. But the pendulum swings, and now as then overexposure to sunshine can bring its dangers. The ancient

Greeks visualised a mediatory god-protector, shielding people, animals and plants from the worst effects of extreme heat. Aristaeus was considered the offspring of Apollo himself, the product of a union between the sun and the clouds. He it was who could command the weather and counter the oppressive heat of a Mediterranean summer by bringing the cool cloudy conditions most favourable to the comfort of humans and the welfare of cattle and sheep, hives of bees, and many growing crops.

In ancient Babylon, where gods and goddesses were numbered by the thousand, a benevolent deity of gentle spring sunshine was revered. He was Asaru, the restorer to happiness and banisher of winter blues. Nowadays people speak of SAD, seasonal affective disorder, and this too has its fashionable peaks and troughs. To counter strong sunshine, the place of Asaru and Aristaeus have been taken by magic potions in jar, tube and bottle, filtering out the harmful excesses of the beloved Apollo.

When the sun is at its seasonal weakest, storms tend to be at their height, and conversely the sun, returning in full strength, could be seen as the mitigator of storms. As their guardian at sea, it was inevitable that Apollo should be especially revered by sailors and fishermen. Apollo could slay the mythical storm dragon Python with a single shaft from his mighty bow. Seagoing men and their families would hold festivals of their own each April, marking the calming of the seas following the winter storms, and celebrating the return of conditions safe enough for them to set out more confidently from their winter harbour.

Nor was it merely sons of toil who venerated the sun. Intellectuals and academics too suffered from SAD: a decline in energy, enthusiasm and general well-being over winter, and they too welcomed the strengthening sunshine of spring with various ceremonies of their own. Apollo, therefore, was also considered a god of intellectual and moral integrity, of civic order and justice; he was also the purifier of penitent souls, and the friend of outcasts and fugitives. He was the god of music and song too, and was closely associated in tradition with the muses of culture, art and science. He was the god of divination and prophecy, provided always that such prophecy was of an ethical nature; dark deeds were not for him! His abiding attribute in the intellectual and moral spheres was his ability to penetrate the darkness of ignorance and superstition and spread enlightenment. His motto, inevitably, was *fiat lux*, let there be light!

As the heavenly being who brought energy to the earth, Apollo has always been thought of as nurturing the qualities of youth and vigour, and regenerative power, and for many centuries his mystical presence was invoked during wedding ceremonies:

Lord Apollo,
Overseer of all,
Be present at the union of this man and this woman.
Let thy light shine in their hearts and loins
And bring their seed to perfection!

This prime giver of strength and energy, of stamina and endurance, has always been revered too by gymnasts and athletes of all kinds. Associated in myth with the names of their classical heroes, Hermes and Hercules, Apollo was invoked by boxers, wrestlers and gladiators before a contest − by all, in fact, who felt they might benefit from an extra reserve of strength.

As everybody's ideal principle of masculine power and beauty, in classical art and sculpture Apollo inevitably is represented as a strong and handsome young man. The symbols traditionally associated with him are the lyre, representing music and culture, the bow, representing power and strength, and a triangle or tripod to represent wisdom and intellectual integrity.

Animals particularly associated with Apollo were the wolf, the dolphin, and the sun-loving snakes. Among birds were the cock, the swan, the hawk, the raven and the crow. Many would say that the teeming world of insects held a special place in Apollo's favours, for more than any other type of creature they are activated by the sun's presence and slowed down by its absence. But among all earth's creatures – perhaps because of the ancient myth of the sun's chariot drawn by fiery white steeds – horses won pride of place as his special favourites. White horses in particular were dedicated to Apollo – indeed, white animals of all kinds have been considered sacred to his name. Chariot races were held at some of his festivals, but in those days of animal-level human souls, the classical days of ancient Greece and Rome, the honour of *victor ludorum* was a dubious one: the winning team was often sacrificed by driving them into deep water to drown.

In classically ancient times several plants were considered sacred to the sun god, under whatever name, particularly the bay laurel, which thrives in hot and dry places. To the priesthood bay foliage was and perhaps still is associated with the expiation of sins. To civic authorities it formed, and sometimes still forms, the famous laurel wreaths presented to heroes, athletes, and others prominent in their field. Also considered sacred to Apollo were the poplar, and the palm tree, which over much of the Middle and Near Eastern world has always been greatly valued for its toughness, its resistance to heat and drought, its welcome shade, and its fruitfulness. Many plants in garden use today seem to enjoy a close relationship with the sun, including sunflowers, Helianthus, Heliopsis, and all other plants named after Helios: the rockrose Helianthemum, the everlasting Helichrysum, the heliotropes; also sun-plants of the genus Portulaca, the sun rose Cistus, the sun-fruit tree, sun cactus, and the sun stocks.

The Sun as a Destiny

It is hardly surprising that among pious people of all races and religions, 'the light' has always been considered the ultimate goal, the hoped-for destiny of human life. From ancient times sages of the Hindu faith have regarded both the sun and the moon as representing human destiny, or as possibly destinations in themselves, with the sun greatly the superior of the two. The earliest of the Upanishads asserts:

DAWN AWAKENING

The lord of creation created two ways: the way of light and the way of reflection. The way of reflection leads to the barren world of the moon. The way of light leads to the sun, to warmth and life.

Some of their prayers, musings and meditations on the glory of the sun variously represent a more philosophical, a more abstract, a more relaxed and yet at the same time more compelling view of the sun's spiritual significance, and are worth recalling:

The sun rises in golden glory, ancient god of all ancient prayers; supreme light and fire, giver of life to all beings. The sun rests on the earthly seasons and shows its glory in a different manner each day.

The sun rises in the east, but its light bathes in life all that is in the east, the south, the west, and the north. The sun gives light and life to all that lives.

Glorious sun, as the seed of life in a mother's womb; the hidden place whence comes the rising sun and the place where it sets; this is all one.

Lord of the sun, of warmth and light; may the rays of your energy which quicken beasts and men, and open the flowers of the garden, long shine on those who adore you!

In his youth the sage meditates on the rising sun, saying: In your rising you bring the promise of life and purification. Include me in your glorious promise.

In his middle years the sage meditates on the noonday sun, saying: You rose in glory to purify the world. Allow me to bask in the blessing of your purification.

In his dying years the sage meditates on the setting sun, saying: You brought hope and glory and purification to the world. Take me with you to the glory of worlds unseen.

Whatever our station in life, our status in society, and whatever our religion, whatever our spiritual orientation, if the opportunity arises to sit quietly and watch the sun's rising before it becomes bright enough to harm the eyes, we should not miss that opportunity. A clear morning, a comfortable spot looking east, preferably from high ground, these are the ideal conditions. Make yourself quiet and peaceful within, banishing thoughts and anxieties as far as possible. Make your mind a blank and receptive screen (without going to sleep), and let the sun's rising fill the emptiness that was left behind as your thoughts and feelings withdrew. The nature of the rising sun can then be felt powerfully in your whole being.

By contemplating the rising sun you may come to feel you are in some way identifying with the earth as it rolls ever eastwards to receive the sun's rays: and indeed this is how it is; the microcosm experiencing the macrocosm. It is not mere imagination: the psychological and the spiritual results are very real, permanent, and undoubtedly beneficial. The practice instils the one passion that can help set the soul on its upward journey, its quest to recapture the long-lost Garden of Eden – the gentle passion of patience combined with faith. If you do not already do this whenever you can, please do so from now on: you *must*!

By the nature of civilised life, far more people are able to watch the setting sun in this way, than the rising sun. The setting sun does not offer quite the same peaceful sense of latent power, however soul-achingly beautiful it may be. Rather than hope and a sure promise of fulfilment, the setting sun seems to express a sense of shortfall, of the urgent *need* for spiritual contact – a need which you should seek to satisfy without delay.

A Lesser Light to rule the Night

So far, we have been considering the sun as a male and the moon as a female principle; most people see it that way. But in the earliest recorded times, it seems, and more recently in the Arab lands, people in the Middle and Near East and much of Europe ascribed these heavenly genders the other way round. Even today it is an Arab trait to see the moon rather than the sun as heavenly controller, and thus masculine: the Arabic and consequently the Moslem year is based on and measured by the cycles of the moon. This of course means that the Moslem calendar seasons are not permanently set in tune with the rest of the world, but cycle too: their New Year, dropping a fortnight annually, ranges with their months through the whole solar year. There are no 'winter months' or 'summer months'. We might surmise that this lunar year is best suited to lands which do not experience positive seasons as distinctive in character as those familiar to the native peoples of Europe and North America. Misunderstandings can arise too, and calculations fly adrift, when a hundred years in one culture equals only ninety-six in another.

Moon as the measurer of time is also, by inference, moon the regulator of lives. In early Babylon certainly it was the moon that ranked as chief among the sky gods. This moon god, the most powerful symbol of divine masculinity, was called Sin, the lord of wisdom, brother god of everybody's mother goddess, Earth. In Arabic lands he was called Wadd, or Nannar the ancient one, or Ammu, divine uncle of all. The great Sin was pictured as an old man with a long beard, and his symbol was a crescent. His wife was none other than the sun goddess, Semes or Samsu, queen of the southern lands.

Archaeology and the study of ancient manuscripts and inscriptions can reveal much of ancient cultures, but after a thousand years of human development seemingly contradictory concepts are uncovered as fashions of thinking change and new beliefs take root. Besides the other deities of the moon in ancient Babylon, we learn of Nusku, god of the new moon considered to be the son of the old moon god Sin. In ancient Egypt, Thoth, the baboon-headed god of learning was (despite his priestly identification with Mercury or Hermes) considered by ordinary people to be god of the moon. In pre-Roman Italy, Summanus was god of the night sky which he patrolled in his moon chariot. And in ancient Scandinavian mythology the youthful god Mani drove the chariot of the moon, while his sister, the beautiful virgin goddess Sol, drove the chariot of the sun.

Quite why it should have been, we cannot tell, but sun and moon changed their genders over the centuries. In Abraham's Chaldean city of Ur the people recognised 'the just laws of Shamash', and by then Shamash, taking over from the sun goddess Semes, had become wholly male, and the moon had adopted a feminine role. But by whichever combination, father-mother or mother-father, sun and moon seem always to have been considered the parents of the planet Venus – the morning star (or equally, the evening star) – otherwise known as the goddess Ishtar. For many centuries, however, people of Arab lands considered the planet Venus too as a male god, giving him the name Athtar.

The majority of Europeans would probably align themselves with St Francis of Assisi when he praised his 'brother sun' and 'sister moon'. But perhaps the Arabs have a point in continuing to consider Venus a male concept: the evening star also symbolises Lucifer, the 'fallen archangel', known after his fall from grace as Satan, governor of the earth and those of earth's inhabitants who are orientated towards materiality.

Almost all the favourite goddesses of classically ancient times have been visualised from time to time as revealing themselves by the light of the moon: Diana, Astarte, Artemis, Juno, Hecate, Selene, Phoebe, Anna Perenna, Cynthia, Dido, Britomartis and Bendis. In the form of diffused light, immediately before rising and after setting, the moon was Hecate, goddess of witchcraft and supernatural events. As a crescent she was Astarte, Juno, or Caelestis, 'the heavenly one'. As the full moon and brilliant moonlight itself, she was Selene or Luna. On wild nights with scudding clouds she was Diana, sometimes called Cynthia, the 'cloud huntress'. Selene too was often seen as a huntress carrying bow and arrows, wearing a golden diadem and driving a chariot drawn by two white horses. Perhaps the name that has been handed down to us as most typical of the moon personified is the Roman Luna, or Noctiluca, 'lamp of the night'. In Egypt she has been identified as Io 'the wanderer', a priestess of Juno who was loved by Jupiter – the human soul – and condemned as a consequence to roam across the face of the earth in the form of a heifer with shining horns, watched over by the many-eyed Argus. Cows have frequently featured in stories of the moon's progress across the sky, their sweeping horns an obvious symbol of the crescent moon itself.

Light pollution is one of the less desirable consequences of our civilisation. It is a price we have to pay for the convenience of having our ways lit at night, a consequence of our feelings of insecurity at having to travel anywhere at night unless the entire area is illuminated with lurid yellow light. It is a bane for anyone wanting to study the stars, for inevitably it blots out all but the very brightest. Anyone who has lived or travelled in sparsely populated parts of the world will appreciate this. The night skies in our civilised lands are a miserable travesty of the glory to be seen elsewhere – the glory to be seen in our own lands not so many years ago. Small wonder then, that the average person nowadays seems to have lost touch with the stars, the planets, the 'heavenly host'. Even the moon often goes unnoticed, unobtrusively pale above the yellow glow rising from the towns and the major highways crossing the countryside between them.

Closely associated with the moon in Roman times, the goddess Anna Perenna, 'the evergreen', was widely believed able to bestow the gift of long life and renewed health on her followers and admirers, in the way that the moon itself is renewed each month. Appropriately enough, her feast was held in the spring during a full moon, when townsfolk and villagers alike would gather in a local orchard when the fruit trees were in blossom. There they would party amid the flowers shining white in the moonlight until the moon had crossed the sky. It was certainly a good excuse for a get-together, but it is equally certain that it could not happen like that today. The modern barbecue would add to the lurid light pollution on all sides, the fruit blossom would appear black in the sodium street lights, and the moon would shine wanly unnoticed.

Moon parties were by no means confined to the followers of official gods and goddesses. The Old Testament has numerous references to the regular feasts and ceremonies of the new moon recognised by the Hebrews. The line between these official ceremonies and the popular moon party was a thin one. Preaching to anyone who would listen the prophet Jeremiah, in the 7th century BC, complained bitterly that, rather than pursue to the letter their exclusive religion as handed down by Moses, the people were following the old pagan custom of honouring the moon and celebrating her cycles. "Do you not see what is taking place in the streets of Jerusalem?" was his lament. "The children are gathering wood, their fathers are kindling fires, and their mothers are kneading dough to make crescent-cakes for the queen of heaven!" A moon feast was a happy family occasion that the common folk did not want to forget. Perhaps they felt that Moses had handed down little in the way of love, or even sentiment. Appreciation of nature's beauty is something that makes the heart grow fonder.

Cakes in the shape of the moon have featured in moonlight ceremonies and parties for thousands of years, and so have round cakes covered with candles to represent the moon's glow. A shadow of this ancient custom is to be seen today in the tradition of lighting candles on a birthday cake. Though the custom has come to mean something different, the ancient hope for stability, for long life and good health has remained unchanged. At heart, perhaps, the sentiment has altered little over the years. The simple enjoyment of a party, an unspoken faith, and the hope of blessings for the future, these things are ageless.

Have we risen above the temptation, then, to worship the hosts of heaven, so real to Bronze Age men, and the concern of Old Testament prophets? I'm afraid not: the more likely explanation is, we have sunk beneath it! To worship such things was symptomatic of Bronze Age spiritual fragmentation. To close them off and not even notice the glory of the skies is symptomatic of the coalition which we have formed with the sophistication of materiality, our own particular brand of spiritual paralysis: that all-consuming materialism from which, from the spiritual point of view, it would be good to escape.

If at all possible, on a clear moonlit night, it is well worth while to take the time and trouble to study the beauty of the moon. Select a place where you can sit undisturbed and meditate with an open mind. Now, as of old, the moon is full of beauty, smoothness, serenity and peace, rewarding her admirers, not merely in a poetic or even a religious sense, but both psychologically and physically. If the moon can raise the surface of the oceans enough to cause tides, drawing an immense weight of water upwards so many feet, as indeed she can, it follows that she must also hold influence over our bodily functions, countering the aging effects of the earth's gravity. When you lay your psyche open to the elements by quietening your thoughts and feelings, the inner self, the soul, will supervise the process. Renewed health and well-being, regularity of metabolic functions and a trouble-free circulation should result. The moon acts as a great balancing wheel for life on earth, and if we are agreeable to helping that balancing process along we shall not be the losers. We shall be in tune with the process of evolution and the natural flow of what has been called the great world dream, culminating in human perfection.

The city moon, the suburban moon, the village moon, the countryside moon, the wilderness moon, they all have subtly different qualities and bestow correspondingly different gifts – of course, because whilst the moon cannot create something new for the body or for the soul, she can and does bring out the qualities and enhance the potentialities that are already there, the different expectations of people with differing lifestyles. The moon has a personal influence on each of us, and it will at least be interesting to put these things to the test of personal experience.

Personalising the Hosts of Heaven

The stars, fixed in their constellations, have always been seen as impersonal overseers of whatever has been ordained by heavenly powers even loftier than they. Human imagination has woven many stories about them, stories of creation and explanations of matters beyond human control. Planets, on the other hand, are mobile, roaming across the fixed background of stars. In earliest times when men first began to domesticate animals, planets were described as celestial sheep straying across the heavens. The bright star Orion was called 'the faithful shepherd of heaven' watching over his flock. As people became more aware of their own individual psychology, discovering 'compartments of awareness' in themselves and others, they associated themselves with these moving points of light as divine reflections of their own fleeting thoughts and feelings, hopes and fears.

Each planet came to represent a particular aspect of the personality, but on an impersonal, macrocosmic scale, and given identities and individuality as gods and goddesses. The planetary deities served to focus and magnify these psychological characteristics. Thus the planet we call Venus, representing emotional feelings, was *all* emotions, through and through. The planet we call Mercury was the epitome of clever thinking, darting with the rapidity of thought and the speed of light between every point of reference, gleaning information and distributing it as he went. Mars, the red planet, was the seat of fierce passions well known to nomadic people trying to carve a niche for themselves in their environment. Jupiter represented the communal human soul at a time when the reality of 'soul' was much closer than now to the common awareness – the highest of human principles, though still subject to the rulership of Saturn, the cyclic principle of harvesting and sowing again in sequence, the principle of time: death, decay, rebirth, new growth.

These were the visible planets – those which could be seen without optical aids. Modern astrology of course follows the same general pattern, but includes the three 'invisible planets', Uranus, Neptune and Pluto (now officially demoted to the status of 'minor planet'). But nowadays, while retaining the basic principles, we tend to give planetary symbolism a far more personal slant. You need have no doubts that planetary astrology does work as a moving plan – a reflection of human affairs. As Carl Gustav Jung put it: "Astrology represents the summation of all the psychological knowledge of antiquity", and he coined the useful term 'synchronicity' to describe the relationships, the mysterious astrological parallels unexplained by science. In *The Secret of the Golden Flower* he wrote: "Astrology is assured of recognition from psychology without further restrictions". Predictive astrology does hold fascination for a great many people. Most indeed would love to see their future, divine the outcome of their actions, see clearly what steps they should take to win success. Having equated the solar system with the human psyche, and having been convinced of the validity of Jungian synchronicity, by whatever name they might have known it, ancient scholars began to put the cart before the horse, to look at the planets, sun and moon as though they were *controlling* human affairs rather than reflecting them.

And so over many centuries the art of predictive astrology steadily grew into the flourishing industry that it is today: part rubbish; part wisdom. The advent of computerised horoscopes has made astrology more and more materialistic, more and more downward-looking, more and more *satanic*. But throughout it all, whether looking up or looking down, it is very plain to see that the whole issue was and still is, unconsciously perhaps, aimed at the same target. This end principle, this burning desire, this unexpressed need is: to know one's own true self; to identify and then penetrate the labyrinth of acquired passions and alien instincts that have obscured the truly human nature, to meet the inner self, and finally to discover the spiritual reality that should be the undisputed leader within our own being. A principle such as this may be expressed in religious terms or in psychological terms, or in every-day common sense terms, but the essence of it has little relationship with religion, psychology, or even common sense. The essence of it is the nature of life itself.

Chapter Three

Ripples of Emotion

STEEP-SIDED LAKES are often described by local inhabitants as 'bottomless' – that is, they seem to be unfathomable. In Italy the Alban hills close to Rome, thrown up by primeval volcanic activity, include spectacular craters some of which have become filled with water over the centuries. One of these flooded craters is Lake Nemi, a three-mile stretch of water that in ancient times was called 'the Mirror of Diana'. The chief shrine of Diana – not only a goddess of nature but the most universally popular of all ancient deities, and known under various names by people of all races, as one to whom they could turn when feeling oppressed or threatened – was situated there amongst the trees, hard against the rocky hillside.

One of Diana's many supernatural guises was the moon – and for many people a sight of the full moon majestic over the darkness of nature still brings her name to mind. At Lake Nemi her beauty on moonlit nights seemed reflected there in the dark water, her expression seeming to change with the moving clouds, a magical mirror framed by the steeply wooded slopes on all sides. From her shrine on such a night, looking down over the water, the supernatural presence of Diana would have seemed almost tangibly real to any emotionally receptive person. In their imagination, visitors at night could well have peopled the lake with naiads, the surrounding woods with dryads and fauns, all the playful aspects perhaps of Diana's own complex temperament, personification of the spirit of wild nature.

Worshippers and family petitioners we are told used to make the pilgrimage from Rome on foot, bringing offerings of flowers and crescent moon-shaped cakes, and little lamps or home-made candles to light in her honour at the shrine. They would follow the famous Appian Way from the capital, turning off after a few miles along a tree-lined side road winding through the Alban hills among mature forests of oak, pine and chestnut. We can imagine their watchful eyes catching the first glint of Diana's lake through the trees, far below them in the steep-sided hollow. Perhaps Diana's worshippers would sit in quiet family groups on the lake shore, rising occasionally to dip their cupped hands in the water and make their supplication:

The lake is full; the moon is full; our hearts are full.
We light a lamp in your honour, O Diana.

This, indeed, is what water can mean to the human heart: the means whereby its own feelings, sentiments, emotions, are reflected back and redoubled. Water tends to have the effect of heightening whatever we are already feeling – thus a stream, a lake, a fountain, a spring, or a waterfall, seen through emotional eyes, can represent in one, sorrow, in another, great love, in yet another, despair; perhaps even hatred and a desire for revenge. Peace of mind is there too, and almost automatically the poetic heart is inspired by water and drawn towards its musical sound and reflected light. If we call upon the muse, or the cultural spirits of water, this is what we are doing: opening and enhancing or expanding our own feelings, whatever they may be.

The Water of Creation

Whether your viewpoint is sentimental or scientific, water is at the very heart and root of life. Traditionally it has been considered one of the four basic elements – fire, earth, air and water – without which there could be no living world, no nature, no plants, beasts or people. Water is constantly reacting with the other elements, soaking the earth and dissolving its salts, trapping with its movements the life-giving oxygen from the air. Water is constantly in circulation, drawn up by the heat of the sun to moisten the atmosphere, falling again in the form of rain, snow, mist or dew.

Water seems somehow older, more primeval, more basic even than solid rock, and ancient creation myths often stress this point. To take the one most familiar to the western world, the biblical Book of Genesis relates how in the beginning:

The earth was without form, and void; darkness was upon the face of the deep. And the Spirit of God moved upon the face of the waters. And God said ... Let there be a firmament in the midst of the waters, and let it divide the waters from the waters. And God made the firmament, and divided the waters which were under the firmament from the waters which are above the firmament.

Ancient creation myths abound. The Babylonian story personifies the elements that existed at the beginning, though the principle is the same as that given in Genesis. Salt water was made to gather beneath the firmament and fresh water above it – which indeed is pretty much the situation to this day. The female principle of primeval chaos that existed before the division between heaven and earth, was visualised as a dragon called Tiamat. Together with Zu, the primeval storm demon, she ruled over the watery chaos. Then came the male principle of fresh water, the god Apsu, who united with Tiamat, and their union gave rise to the countless minor gods of heaven and earth recognised by the Babylonians, and all these beings worked to create order, each in their own specialised field. Tiamat became the supreme goddess of salt water on earth; Apsu became the supreme god of fresh water, and the ruling god of the sky. The storm demon Zu and his numerous assistants were driven off to become the constellations.

Even at the sheerly practical, material level of understanding about water – whether it is the life-saving water which is there to drink and on which we all depend, or whether it is the nuisance-value water which floods and makes you uncomfortably wet when it rains, there is always a depth of feeling attached to it. Even on a strictly utilitarian basis involving canals, reservoirs, taps, faucets, hydrants, bowsers and sewage works, the life-sustaining properties of water ensure that the most unromantic-seeming appearance of water can hold wonder and beauty in the eyes of any person willing to see it. There is a place for water in the soul, somewhere between the instinctual human and material levels of being: a place where the imagination is inspired to produce all manner of completely non-scientific impressions, images and apparitions. For instance, this is what an old lady once told me:

"I was a passenger on a coach on the way back home from an outing, and we stopped for traffic lights, or something like that, and we were just opposite a sewage works. A whiff of it came through the open window and some of the other people on the coach were complaining and joking about it. The sun was very low in the sky as it was late afternoon, and it was shining on those round pond things they have, with water sprayers going slowly round and round, and I seemed to see these shimmering figures dancing over the water. I've never seen anything so beautiful. Above all those ugly pipes and concrete things there were these wonderful gossamer figures with wispy flowing dresses, all gracefully moving and dancing over the water. I've never told anyone about it before. They'd think I was mad!"

The others on the coach of course could see no more than the play of sunlight on moving jets of water. Because most people are firmly centred in the material level of emotional understanding, where a spade is rarely more than just a spade, very few are able to see mystical beauty transforming the workaday scene. This is the same level of creative story-telling from which in ages past sprang tales and legends of nymphs, mermaids, sea serpents and kelpies. It is the process of spiritual fragmentation being experienced by a human soul on the path of descent, at a time (in personal if not in general human history) when primal oneness had been lost, but the down-to-earth realism of solid materiality had not yet been fully gained. At this level of the psyche, symbols become a way of analysing the varied perceptions of the mind.

Purely natural phenomena on occasions can also give rise

to supernatural imaginings. For instance, I was walking over a Scottish hill on one occasion and was passing a little reservoir pond when there was a 'plop', and the water within a small area began bubbling and stirring as though on the boil. Gurgling like a pulled bath plug the water began to swirl, rising a foot or two up from the surface. I thought for a moment that there must be a pipe outlet which had suddenly opened, but no; the miniature whirling column moved swaying over the surface of the pond growing steadily taller and taller, seeming to take on a living form. As it reached the edge of the pond it disappeared, leaving only ripples behind.

I wondered how it might have looked by moonlight – surely a ghostly sight. A kelpie playing in the water perhaps, a water demon, a malicious sprite said to take the form of a horse rearing from the water and liable to strike down any passer-by who ventures recklessly close. For as the Scottish lyrical poet W. S. Graham wrote: 'Every lake has its kelpie, often seen ... dancing along the surface of the deep, or browsing upon the pasture on its verge'. For me, however, the mystery was solved as the column of energy continued across land in the form of a small whirlwind, sending dead grass and thistledown spinning high in the air. I had witnessed the birth – albeit short-lived – of a potential water spout.

Full sized water spouts – or twisters at sea – give an idea of the force for destruction that water can become: a truly awesome spectacle, threatening when you find yourself in a vulnerable situation, perhaps in a small boat, even a large ship, or even on dry land at the edge of the sea. As the equivalent of a tornado on land, a wholly unstoppable force has been unleashed. If a reasonable-sized tornado had indeed passed across that pond, the water and everything in it would probably have been sucked up, no doubt to fall elsewhere as rain: hence perhaps the mysterious reports of it raining fish or frogs, that we hear about from time to time.

The sea of course holds massive emotional appeal, and possibly a healing influence for stressed-out minds. Why else would normally land-locked people make a long journey in order to sit for hours on end staring out to sea, or listening with closed eyes to the soothing murmur of waves stirring the shingle, whispering on the sand? It can only be because these are sights and sounds which soothe the anxious heart and really seem to replenish the soul in some way. Somehow, the sea seems to offer the *answer*, even though the question itself is unformulated and unclear.

It is this sense of potency, besides the obvious material power that the sea is capable of exerting, that have helped to give rise to the innumerable myths and fables and fairy stories based on this theme. The folklore tales of the Grimm brothers have the one about the fisherman who lived with his wife in a hovel near the sea. He caught an enchanted fish, and then released it when it spoke to him, but his greedy wife made him go back and ask the fish to give them a nice cottage to live in – a reasonable enough request. This was granted, but not content with that she sent her husband back again and again to demand a series of favours, each more outrageous than the last: to be king, to be emperor, to be pope. All these were within the fish's power and thence within the power of the sea to grant, for they were but the material boons of the world. But when she demanded to be made lord and ruler of the sun and moon, the fish withdrew all the favours that had been granted and returned them to their original poverty. The sea with all that live in it represents the emotions, and the emotional heart with its desires is limited to earth, to materiality, to this earthly life. The supernatural power she wanted for herself had broken the spell and brought her back to the reality of earth.

By way of human imagination inspired by the sea, and the 'wild white horses' of breaker and spume, creatures of the deep have inevitably been ascribed mystical powers, in the spirit of Shakespeare's 'sea change into something rich and strange'. But there is more to it than this. Once such a being has been established in the heart, it can inspire religious certainty and a reverential sense of awe. Grimm's household tales are full of such semi-solid beings, the bit-part players of ancient religions.

To the Babylonians, for instance, Oannes was a perfectly solid god who lived in the sea, with a man's body and a fish's head, visualised as clever and influential, a patron of arts and science. Conversely Triton, to the ancient Greeks, was a sea god with a fish's body and a man's head, and it was he who created the roaring of the waves by blowing on a conch shell. Another sea god, Glaucous, 'the blue-grey one', was depicted as a wild old man with a fish's tail and scales of the greyish blue-green that gave him his name. He had long hair and a beard like seaweed flowing in the water, and his body too was decorated with seaweed and shells. He was usually accompanied by a retinue of nereid sea-nymphs. He was indeed very similar in concept to Nereus, 'the old man of the sea', the supposed father of the nereids, and he too was visualised with flowing seaweed hair. Another 'old man of the sea' was the god Proteus, able at will to assume any shape he chose, or indeed to become shapeless, rather like the sea from which he rose. He was credited with being the protector of seals, and any other mammals able to hide in the sea.

The classical Greek god of the sea, and all other watery places, was Poseidon, the father of Triton, and ultimately the same character as the Roman Neptune. Like Neptune he bore a trident and was closely associated with horses which were considered sacred to his name. Neptune's chariot was depicted being drawn through the waves by a monstrous sea horse – the hippocampus, with a horse's head, mane and forelegs, and the powerful hindquarters and tail of a gigantic fish. In stormy weather Poseidon is symbolised by a black bull, snorting and charging, signifying his fiercely dark moods. In fair weather his symbol is the dolphin, friendly and playful.

Then there is Palaemon or Melicertes, and Portunus, Melkart, Sozon, and Oceanus who in the mythology of the Greeks was depicted as an old man with bull's horns. Amongst all the races of mankind, there have probably been hundreds of sea gods, which modern minds would dismiss as mere products of the superstitious imagination of sea-faring folk. But they are products of the heart –

of the deepest feelings. In dreams and visions the heart can be seen personified, playing the role that best befits the emotions of the hour. They are more than mere imagination: they have reality because they belong to the fundamental nature of their beholder's heart.

Pacifying the waves

People who make a precarious living at sea, or who follow a trade at the water's edge, know only too well how changeable the sea can be: its moods like the human heart itself can alter rapidly from peaceful to furious and back again. The more furious the sea, inevitably, the more masculine its associations. The more peaceful it seems, the more feminine its personification. The beautiful goddess Venus or Aphrodite, or Anadyomene who rose from the sea, under the masculine name of Aphroditos or Hermaphroditos, has even been depicted in art and sculpture wearing a beard, as though to indicate her unpredictable inconsistency, her rapid changes from the feminine to the masculine mode of expression. The principle of intercession, calling hopefully upon a kind goddess to plead with a furious sea god for the merciful abatement of a storm, is an irresistible one; a hermaphrodite intermediary takes the principle a stage further.

Goddesses of the sea too are numerous, and as often as not of a national or even of a local nature. Local sea goddesses may well have had their origin in the story of some local heroine: one such is Leucothea, the 'white goddess' of the Mediterranean. Her ancient story tells how, as a human mother, she leapt into the sea with her child to escape the attentions of a madman. She and the baby were rescued and brought to a safe part of the shore by friendly dolphins, and ever after she was revered by sailors and fishermen as a goddess. Her son, growing up, became Portunus, the harbour god – perhaps the least masculine and least furious of all the sea gods – whose self-imposed duty it was to see ships safely into port, to act himself as the friendly dolphin who shepherds human lives inshore.

There can be few sights more peacefully beautiful than that of dolphins or porpoises playing in the calm sea, and these creatures have won a place in the hearts of countless generations of men – except perhaps in those hard-edged lands where these seemingly noble creatures are periodically rounded up by fishermen and slaughtered. The nature of sentimentality has a markedly racial variability. But in the Mediterranean area in classical times (where the sun, personified as Apollo, was seen as the prime mover in the abatement of wintry storms) seaside communities recognised the *delphinia* ceremonies – spring festivals praising the spirit of the dolphin and given in honour of Apollo, offering thanks for the calming of the seas after the rough weather of winter, enabling sailors and fishermen to venture out more freely in their frail boats.

But of course, with or without a place for dolphins, heartfelt ceremonies with thousand-fold variations have been held on a thousand coast lines during the ages. The symbolism, the manner of projection of each community's shared feelings will differ, but the need is the same. Alongside the Aegean Sea, the goddess of fishing and navigation was Brizo, the guardian deity of sailors honoured especially by the seamen's wives, who would intercede on their behalf when Poseidon was in one of his dark moods. Brizo's worshippers would prepare portions of food which they consecrated to the goddess by setting them afloat on the sea in miniature boats made of sticks and leaves.

The contents of such festivals and the hopes of the people who take part in them are perhaps little different from those of more modern times who may sometimes gather close to the harbour wall to sing:

> *Eternal Father, strong to save,*
> *Whose arm hath bound the restless wave,*
> *Who bidd'st the mighty ocean deep*
> *Its own appointed limits keep;*
> *O hear us when we cry to Thee*
> *For those in peril on the sea.*

RIPPLES OF EMOTION

In the hearts of those who repeat their prayers and sing their songs with sincerity, there is no real difference between the various names and powers called upon to represent the elements. Without disrespect to the traditions of Christianity, the sentiment is the same: the wish to evoke the possibility of a boon, a grace, an act of mercy.

In many parts of the ancient world the 'people's favourite goddess', Diana, who often went under her Greek alias of Artemis, was thought to rise from her favourite forests and range over the sea by way of the moon. Certainly she was called upon routinely by seafarers of the Aegean and Mediterranean to grant them safe and prosperous sea voyages. She too was associated with the dolphins of fair weather, and given the title Delphinia, assuming her to be the consort of Delphinius, the Greek god of estuaries and inshore seas, and thence of the dolphins – and as many sailors will have it even today (if only tongue-in-cheek), dolphins themselves are said to be the reincarnations of drowned sailors.

But the truly sea-born goddess, fabled to have risen out of the sea near the Cypriot shore, was of course Aphrodite, also known as Venus Anadyomene, and whom we have already noted could at will take on the enigmatic guise of Hermaphroditos. Everywhere seashells were arranged as decorative symbols of Aphrodite in little shrines among the rocks of the seashore. She had many names and many guises, many personalities, and a separate title to cover every function she was called upon to perform. When sought by mariners to protect them from rough seas, she was Galenia, or 'fair weather'. To merchant seamen setting out on a venture she was Euploia, 'prosperous voyages'. And when disaster struck and ships foundered, she was Muchia, 'goddess of the depths'. and Melainis, 'the dark one', wearing a widow's veil to signify her connection with death and burial, and loved ones lost at sea.

Sailors and fishermen of Scandinavia and the northern lands had even more cause to be wary of the sea and its moods than had their southern counterparts. Their supreme sea goddess was Niordhir, who reached out of the mist and concealed her form with sea-fog. In northern lands, inevitably, frost has always been personified among the gods and goddesses thought able to influence the weather. The Scandinavian frost god, or supernatural frost-giant carrying a club of ice, is Gymir – Jack Frost sounds more familiar in English – and he was married to the fertility goddess Freyr. Their beautiful but cold daughter was the nymph-like frost goddess Gerda: the fair skin of Gerda's naked arms and her pure white dress together shone so brightly that both sea and air were illuminated with a brilliant white glow, enough to dazzle sailors many miles off shore. This dazzle is a real phenomenon, by the way, one which warns seamen of dangerous ice ahead, and known to them as 'ice-blink'.

The Weather for Romance

Hera, the queen of heaven, may not still be invoked in the mountains when rain is urgently needed, but she is still official keeper of the clouds; they are her special responsibility. As fleeting clouds range across the open sky or scud across the face of the moon (whence they are chased by the 'cloud huntress' Cynthia), it is the great Hera herself who decides whether or not rain will fall that night. The seven nymphs of the rain, the hyades, can do nothing but watch and wait hopefully from their home in the constellation Taurus.

In the West, Thor and the other storm gods may be outmoded. But what's in a name? Hadad, also known as Rimmon, Ramman, or Adduramman, the eastern storm god, prince of cloudbursts and thunderstorms, is ageless, unlimited by time or space. The dry back seat of your car may seem an ideal spot for courting in the rain, but beware: someone up there takes perverse delight in bogging down your carriage – setting your wheels spinning in the mud, and summoning various demons of the night to gloat over your plight.

The bogeyman is a fairly universal frightener for naughty children who will not settle down for the night. The Babylonians went a step further: from their pantheon, or pandemonium, they produced Lilith, a fearful vampire demon of the night who makes her appearance mainly in stormy weather. As she roams looking for victims, children wandering on their own were thought to be in particular danger from her attentions. She or her sisters may still be around (indeed, there are signs that she, now in the 21st century, is coming back into fashion), socialising perhaps with the frightful skeletal kergrims and other undead friends. Watch out for the flapping of her black robes, and listen for her blood-chilling wail, the next time you walk through a graveyard on a stormy night.

Storms cannot simply happen. They are brought by the wind, and the winds which bring storms may well have been conjured up by Enlil, lord of the fierce winds. But the gentler winds that later disperse the storm leaving only freshness in its wake, are sent by the mother of winds – none other than the beautiful Aurora, goddess of dawn, bringing 'the innocent brightness of a newborn day'. It depends upon where you live, of course: prevailing winds and changes of wind direction are associated with specific seasons and different local expectations. In northern Europe the east wind can be bitter and cruel; but further south the east wind personified as Euros by the ancient Greeks, closely connected with the rising sun and thence with the goddess of dawn, was the harbinger of fair weather. Zephyrus, as the mild moist west wind, was messenger of spring, promoting the healthy growth of plants; tellingly, he was also known as Favonius, 'the favourable one', fertiliser of spring flowers, fabled lover of Flora, the goddess of spring. Notus, the south wind, can be hot and dry; Boreas, the north wind, can herald the cold touch of autumn almost anywhere in the northern hemisphere.

All these fanciful names from long ago seem somehow people-friendly: they sprang from the feelings then, and our present-day feelings can be equally open to them. A kind of elemental communication, a natural rapport, can build itself up between the weather and anyone who is constantly aware of it. The direction of the wind can become instinctively known to you, particularly if your livelihood depends on it in some way. A suburban householder can hear which side of the house, which door and which windows are being rattled and pelted with rain during the night, and he can say: "Ah, it's from the north tonight", and sleep easy. He will have become akin to the legendary North American tribesman who is said to have welcomed the icy north wind to his bosom as a living friend.

In Middle Eastern and Mediterranean lands there is rarely a shortage of light. In Scandinavia and all other northern lands, however, light can seem a commodity in short supply, even during the season of the midnight sun, and valued correspondingly highly. The Scandinavian god of light, Heimdall, was said to guard the rainbow bridge to heaven. Certainly, there can be no rainbow without light, and no rainbow without rain − or at least plentiful moisture in the atmosphere. According to the Book of Genesis, the first ever rainbow was set in the clouds as a covenant between God and Noah after the great flood, and according to the Revelation of John the Divine there is a rainbow round about the throne of God. Certainly, there is no more beautiful phenomenon of the weather. In Hindu sacred writing the rainbow is related to the concept of ultimate oneness, and an expression of faith:

Through grace, the mystery of vision transforms the radiance of pure white light into the colours of the rainbow. As all colours originate in pure white light, and to pure white light they surely return, so all God's creatures originate in God, and to God they shall surely return.

According to European classical mythology, the nymph or goddess of the rainbow is Iris. She was considered the virgin messenger of all other gods and goddesses, borne aloft with golden wings, and carrying the staff of Hermes, her unique position expressed by the arc of the rainbow which, spanning the skies, unites heaven and earth. We should never tire of such natural beauty while we live; the rainbow simply invites a poetic sentiment, and as Wordsworth put it:

> *My heart leaps up when I behold*
> *A rainbow in the sky:*
> *So was it when my life began;*
> *So is it now I am a man;*
> *So be it when I shall grow old.*
> *Or let me die!*
> *The Child is father of the Man;*
> *And I could wish my days to be*
> *Bound each to other by natural piety.*

From Flood to Fountain

In many countries of the world agriculture has depended upon an annual flood, usually following torrential rain (or sometimes spring snow-melt) in far-off mountains: along the banks of the lower Nile, for instance, where the goddess Isis, as 'lady of the flood', was and perhaps still is thought responsible for controlling the annual flow of water and the consequent well-being of her people. Without their annual floods the Mesopotamians too – ancient Babylonians and Assyrians – would probably have starved, and they gave the title 'lord of the flood' to Tammuz, their god of dormant vegetation relating to the ongoing cycle of nature.

But there is a world of difference between a life-giving flood which irrigates your fields, and a devastating flood which washes away your painstakingly nurtured topsoil and precludes any kind of cultivation. It can mean the loss of home and possessions, followed by certain famine. The immense difference between the two has often been expressed in myths and fables – as in the story of Achelous, the god of rivers and flood plains (and the name of a river in Greece) who was said to appear in various guises: sometimes as a snake, or a bull, or more commonly as a bull-faced man. In this last guise he had the misfortune to break off one of his horns during a fight with Heracles over a woman, thus losing half of his potency. But in place of the missing horn he was given a cornucopia – a horn of plenty – by the kindly nymph-goddess Amalthea. Amalthea was the goddess of milk and milkmaids who, along with her sister Melissa, the goddess of honey, bees and beekeepers, presided over the proverbial 'land flowing with milk and honey'. And so Achelous, god of the river flood, was left with two distinct sides to his personality: the one reflects the blind ferocious onslaughts of a bull, the other signifies the benign supply of plentiful food, corn, vegetables and fruit from his constantly self-replenishing cornucopia. The image of Achelous neatly sums up the hopes and fears of the peasant farmer struggling to make ends meet on the river plain.

The pre-English British Celts, during their long and ongoing history, have seldom been short of rain to water their fields, but they too have always enjoyed an almost supernatural relationship with their rivers, and with the nymph-goddesses who are said to live in them and help regulate their flow. Sabrina was the Roman name for the Celtic river-nymph Sabre or Hafren of the River Severn, but it was the river god Lud who presided over the water meadows and flood plains of the lower Severn, and provided the best grazing for cattle and horses.

The Celts love horses, and these noble animals are firmly connected with running water in the Celtic mind. Rhiannon is a Celtic goddess of horse-riding, and the domestication of animals in general. Incidentally she is also the patroness of marriage relationships, happy families, and peaceful homely pursuits. She it is who sprinkles dew to moisten the pasturelands on clear mornings, but above all she is a river deity, especially potent at the point where the river runs into its estuary and thence into the sea. Her association with the wild white horses of waves breaking on the shore in a gale, is compelling.

The same could be said of the goddess Epona, though as a river goddess she is more closely connected with the source – with springs and waterfalls – than is Rhiannon. She shares the same intimate love of horses however, and in Celtic art she has sometimes been depicted cast in bronze in the form of a horse, or sometimes as a helmeted maiden riding bareback, as a decoration for amulets, shields or brooches. The mythical kelpie of course is often visualised in the form of a horse, but unlike the gentle Epona and Rhiannon, this Celtic water sprite has been thought of as a malicious creature, one who delights in drowning mortals, sometimes by feigning friendship and luring passers-by onto its back before galloping with them into deep water, and perhaps endangering real flesh and blood horses too, by tempting them to plunge in to the undertow out of their depth.

When the Romans took charge of Celtic river estuaries and sailed their boats upstream to supply their bases, they built shrines to their own gods and goddesses, and in rivers they could see a connection with Janus, their god of doorways – the one who could look both ways at once – patron of all who entered or departed. In the case of Sabrina's river the Severn, it certainly flowed out, but flowed in again with the impressive Severn bore, with its regular backwash carried many miles upstream. The Roman name Janus is the same as Dianus, which in turn is the masculine form of Diana, our familiar 'people's favourite' goddess.

One of the numerous titles bestowed on Diana was Limnaia – 'the lady of the lake', and she was considered chief goddess of the band of nymphs and water sprites which have for many centuries been associated with almost any sheet of water you care to name, especially perhaps if it is surrounded by forest. Not only will the trees make Diana, as the primal supernatural huntress, feel at home; the forest verge is the natural haunt of lustful satyrs who love to gaze on the nymphs as they bathe and dance at the water's edge. Wanton they may be, and passion-ridden, but they are all cheerful, unlike the mournful spirits said to haunt those lakes which are completely in the open. Trees act as natural cloaks, amoral, but soul-warming and spirit-raising. This is especially true of well-matured trees, those which have found their own peace and no longer need to struggle with their fellows for a place in the sun.

OUR SPIRITUAL JOURNEY

The mud of the estuary has never been a likely haunt of nymphs, though other supernatural creatures may well have roamed these wastes. Salt marshes, like other coastal sites, more sea than land, are practical places for practical people who look out to sea for their livelihoods. But freshwater marshes, wild and uninhabited by men, have always been thought a favourite playground of the 'wild wanderer' Diana. Indeed, yet another of her titles is Heleia, 'lady of the marsh'. Marshlands have often been thought to be haunted, sometimes by spectral hounds, sometimes by the ghosts of lost travellers; and of course they are still the undisputed home ground of will o' the wisp, also known as jack o' lantern, or ignis fatuus – the light of a somewhat mysterious nature, spectral or gaseous, reputed to lure unwary travellers to their doom. Whether the real will o' the wisp is composed of methane, spontaneously combusted, or phosphorescence resulting from decaying flesh beneath the surface, it is certainly an organic phenomenon. In years gone by this strange manifestation has been seen in churchyards too, hovering over recent graves: a great source of superstitious imaginings.

The saying 'still waters run deep' has never been more apt than when it is taken to refer to the unconscious mind, the dark workings of the hidden personality beneath the level of conscious awareness. This symbol was probably unknown to anybody who lived before the coming of psychotherapy early in the 20th century, and indeed such deep levels of hidden mind-content are largely the products of our civilisation. The mythical creatures of the underworld relate to the inner selves approaching soul level, rather than that which we have come to think of as the level of psychology, the products of our minds rather than our hearts. The conscious mind has been expressed as a water lily floating on murky waters, feeding and flourishing on the repressed contents of the personal unconscious. Jung's collective unconscious mind too has been described as a vast sea: but even these immense concepts are shallow when compared with the myth-creating depths of the inner self.

A Celebration of Nymphs

The time is ripe to recall fondly the friendly spirits of unpolluted water, guardian goddesses of nature: the dryads and hamadryads of the forest, the oreads of the mountains, the oceanids and nereids of salt water, the naiads of fresh water. Some of their stories may have meaning for us today. Others again may have been purely sentimental – like that of the river nymph Dido who (so it was said by the Romans) put in an appearance, shimmering beneath the surface, only when her sister the moon was to be seen in the sky above. But most are green stories, based on ecological observation, environmental concern. The nymph Syrinx, for instance, was pursued lustfully by Pan and hid in the river. When the gods saw her hiding, in order to save her modesty they changed her into the reeds from which Pan later made his pipes. Castalia too, a nymph who dwelt in a spring on Mount Parnassus, was pursued too avidly by the sun god Apollo, and leapt into the water to escape his overpowering passion. In her case the gods changed her into a water lily. It is streamside vegetation, lush greenery, that helps keep water from excessive evaporation, and their oxygenating properties which purify it and allow people and the animals represented by Pan to use it safely.

Then there is the nymph Daphne, who was pursued so persistently by Apollo that, to protect her virginity, the other gods changed her into the bay laurel – a true plant of the sun ever after held sacred to the name of Apollo. It has been said that a few bay leaves placed under your pillow as you sleep will lend you the gift of prophecy. The sight and sound of water gushing from the ground in spring or fountain is irresistibly associated in our minds, perhaps unconsciously, with new understandings, inspiration and prophecy; with blessings, marriage and fulfilment; with new life, successful childbirth. Is it any wonder that folk-lore has peopled such places with semi-divine beings able to help those who invoke them and drink their water with a sense of reverence? The least we can do is to take care not to pollute their home.

There can be few natural springs that have not at some time been associated with a supernatural presence: a nymph, a sprite, a goddess, a god, a muse, or a human saint following some miraculous enterprise. Holy wells abound, and in such places it has been considered a serious offence to pollute the water. To modern sophisticated minds all sources of fresh water are now particularly to be shielded from harm. We know only too well from our own experience, the ills and misfortunes that can result from pollution, whether careless or malicious.

The Romans, to be on the safe side perhaps, tended to ascribe an individual god or goddess to whatever subject or theme seemed of special importance at the time. A Roman housewife knitting or weaving a garment might conceivably have prayed: 'O Wool, please hear my prayer and see that my husband's new tunic fits him well!' It was an acknowledgement of the spiritual foundation beneath all things, while at the same time focusing the concentration. Following this principle, Fontus was the official Roman god of fountains, springs and wells. Festivals called *fontinalia* were held in his honour at the end of summer, when garlands were ceremoniously cast into the city fountains or set to float on village wells. If the well was too deep, flowers would be arranged around the top. From these beginnings we can trace the origins of the well-decorating ceremonies which are still held in rural communities around the world today, usually with a local fable to augment the custom.

In the classical European world, nymphs and goddesses were as numerous as the springs, streams, wells and fountains which they inhabited, and one of the best-known was Egeria, goddess of 'issuing forth' from the source, whether referring to the water of springs or fountains, or the new life of childbirth. The famous vestal virgins used to journey from the city of Rome to carry water for their temple ceremonies from Egeria's spring close to Diana's shrine at Lake Nemi. Egeria, who reputedly was able to offer wise counsel to all worthies and government officials who requested it, was even asked on occasion to give advice to the emperor himself. A pretty little brown and gold butterfly which inhabits sunlit woodland glades and is often found near water, has been named after Egeria.

Childbirth, new life issuing forth, was associated with springs and fountains in both the Roman and Greek traditions. Niobe was the Greek personification of a mother's sorrow at the death of her children, an all-too-common event, and was seen as a stone in the spring, constantly shedding tears. Two or three butterflies have been named after Niobe, for their dark and tear-stained appearance and waterside habitats, and a delicate white butterfly has been named after Aganippe; she was a water nymph who dwelt in a spring held sacred to the muses, and through this association was considered the guardian nymph of poetic inspiration − not the muse of poetry herself, but the inspiration supplied by the sound of gently running water.

The actual muse of poetry, herself guardian goddess of a sacred spring and the noblest of the muses, was Calliope, 'she of the fair voice', and in her honour yet another butterfly has been named: this time a beautiful crimson one. The muses represented culture in the ancient world, and culture inevitably has been associated with water and the sound of water. They were conceived by human soul out of memory, the nine daughters of Zeus and Mnemosyne. Besides Calliope there is Euterpe, 'she that gladdens', a nymph-goddess set to guard a sacred spring from whence men drew inspiration, and the muse of music and song − the favourite muse of Apollo, incidentally, to whom music was especially dear.

Then there was Erato, 'the lovely one' again originally a nymph of the fountain, who became a goddess of inspiration and the muse of erotic poetry − of love poems. Then of course there are Clio, the muse of history; Thalia, the muse of dramatic comedy and pastoral poetry; Melpomene, the muse of dramatic tragedy; Terpsichore, the muse of dancing and lyric poetry; Polyhymnia, the muse of harmony, music and singing; and Urania, the muse of astrology and celestial knowledge, and the inspiration to be gained perhaps by watching stars sparkle in the water.

All these things are from the heart, and for the heart: the seat of sincerity, the seat of religious fervour, the seat of desire, the seat of deception, of arrogance and fanaticism. All the nicenesses and all the nastinesses of human society, all are from the heart. The fervour of men's hearts, taken to extremes, can make even the noblest of religions seem like something vile. As the prophet Jeremiah pointed out in his own uncompromising way: "The heart is deceitful above all things, and desperately wicked". But no matter how wicked, no matter how sincere and noble, no matter how sure, all this will change. One thing is certain: the heart cannot carry the soul into the realms of spirit. The heart lives in the world of nature, and remains tied to the world of earth and water.

CHAPTER FOUR

Deep Waters of Spirit

HAVING EXPLORED some of the many ways by which water can symbolise the human heart with its emotions, we can readily appreciate how it can be used to symbolise something at a much higher level in the scheme of things, something from beyond the range of thoughts and feelings, something from the dawn awakening of what we might call the great world dream – something from the realm of spirit. As an earthly symbol of something fluid, intangible and non-material, water is the nearest thing we can find, the idea that lies behind the principles of holy water and the baptism. Just as life itself depends on the presence of water, so water can symbolise the power of life itself: the river of life. The idea is to be found reflected in the Svetasvatara Upanishad, from which many have drawn spiritual inspiration over the centuries, visualising the human soul searching the murky and dangerous waters of the passions, hopefully seeking contact with the peaceful waters and the initiating rites of spirit:

In meditation a wise man saw the river of life rushing in full spate, flowing from a fountain of consciousness; fed by five turbid tributaries of the senses, with high waves whipped up by the winds of passionate breath; with five great whirlpools full of sorrow and loneliness, and five rocky ravines echoing with danger and pain.

Along the turgid river of life flies a solitary swan with whistling wings: the human soul seeking quiet waters on which to rest. While she flies with a restless heart she despairs of finding peace; but when Spirit guides she is shown a tranquil lake with clear water and sheltering reeds.

Expressions of symbolic awareness such as this may or may not be meaningful to Hindus today, but it is of little use taking the images of one religion or another in order to describe the spiritual cataract, the fish-ladder of souls, the means of ascent that really does exist on the inner plane, because that would be to invite invidious comparisons with other religions and ways. As you may have noticed, very religious people tend to suppose – to believe – that their own religion comprises spiritual reality in fact, rather than a symbol of that reality, and it is always best not to argue with a religious point of view.

It is far safer to use religious ideas from long ago, from a religion which no longer has adherents, and which can no longer cause offence. That is why I shall take the Euphrates of the Babylonians as my example of a 'sacred river'. The identification of water with 'spirit', as an earthly symbol of supernatural presence, has been the instinctive assumption of men since the earliest written words were made permanent.

Now Babylon has acquired a very bad name over the millennia which have elapsed since its heyday, mainly because of the indignation caused by the defeat and occupation of Israel at the hands of Nebuchadnezzar, the kidnapping and exile of Israeli skilled workers and intellectuals as virtual slaves of the Babylonians, and the fact that it was all recorded and given a very 'bad press' in the Old Testament. But the Babylonian symbols of spirituality were instinctively sound, though overlaid with what may seem to us the childlike superstitions of their day.

Virtually every trace of the ancient cities has disappeared over the millennia, but hard-baked clay lasts, and thousands of cuneiform clay tablets have been unearthed by archaeologists, especially from beneath what must have been the city records office and public library of their day. Most of what is known of the city-state of Babylon came from the information on these tablets. They tell, for instance, of a great annual ceremony involving King Nebuchadnezzar and his priests during which they followed and re-enacted their own symbolic spiritual ascent known to them as "the sacred path of Marduk".

DEEP WATERS OF SPIRIT

Babylonians were probably the first to isolate traits of human psychology, to relate these to the planets, and to personify these planet symbols as gods and goddesses. But they went a step further than that, and in the spirit of 'as above, so below', the land they lived in was made to reflect this system on a different scale. The very name 'Babylon' has come to imply an excess of materiality, wealth and luxury, and shameless idolatry. The name comes from the phrase 'Gateway to God', and much of Babylonian history justifies this title. The gateway, a means of passing through to a different spiritual dimension, has to function by way of the soul. Only soul can be instrumental in bringing about a spiritual encounter. It is patently true that the concept of 'God' will have to include materiality as well as spirituality, but only spirit can activate spirit or approach matters of spirit; and spirit within the human sphere has to function by way of the soul − by activating the soul which may well have lain dormant for many years. 'Spirit' must not be confused with emotion. Spirit is not to be known by science; not to be discovered by clever minds.

Nebuchadanezzar and his priestly hierarchy may not have been clever by our modern standards − they would probably be seen today as thick as the proverbial two short planks. Neither were they saintly people − far from it. But they were aware of an all-important principle all but lost today: the principle that soul represents the way to a higher condition; the understanding that soul must be allowed to lead if that condition is to be gained.

Babylon itself was the city-state which ruled the land of Mesopotamia, the area between the two major rivers of the Tigris and the Euphrates, and equating to modern Iraq. The civic motto of the city of Babylon was 'Marduk is Bel' − 'the soul is lord'. Their city name, 'Gateway to God', takes the matter a stage further, for if the city of Babylon represented the soul as symbolised by Jupiter, the other sister cities of the Mesopotamian plain each represented another, essential if less exalted, part of the human organism. These different 'rulers' of the human condition in their turn were symbolised by idols − given solidity of form − perhaps so that the uneducated masses would have some inkling of the principles involved. That simple fact has caused righteous indignation and moral outrage in people who happened to use a different set of symbols; people who thought that their own religious symbols were the only true symbols – or even that *their* symbols were not symbols at all, but spiritual reality itself.

Babylon, then, city of a thousand idols, was in fact the city of the soul. For everyday government, for kings and councillors, the highest recognised authority was symbolised by Shamash, the sun: the spirit of openness and justice whose light shines on all, who exposes misdeeds and uncovers evil, the champion of triumphal careers, patron of all outward accomplishments of the rich and famous. Worldly success, for Babylonians, belonged to Shamash; spiritual progress belonged to Marduk. Shamash with his 'just laws' ruled over the outer self, the physical and moral actions of the people. Marduk ruled over the inner self.

Whilst Babylon itself honoured Marduk, the other cities of the Mesopotamian plain each honoured their own personal deity, symbolised by their idols. The city of Borsippa, ten miles away to the south-west on the banks of the Euphrates, was the home ground of Nabu or Nebu (the one we know as Mercury), representative of thoughts – the intellectual centre. A similar distance away to the north-east, the city of Cuthah honoured the warlike Nergal (known to us as Mars), ruler of the passions and the dreaded one who takes command of the underworld (for this is certainly where the passions ultimately lead). For this reason the city of Cuthah was known throughout the region as 'the assembly-place of ghosts'. It was also the martial centre for the region, the garrison town of Nebuchadnezzar's crack troops.

The patron-god of Lagash, many miles away on the edge of the Sumerian salt marshes, was Ninurta (known to us as Saturn). This was a desolate place associated in the Babylonians' minds with death and dissolution. The great goddess Ishtar (Venus), seat of emotions, was particularly venerated in the city of Erech, again far to the south. The Euphrates had changed its course at least a thousand years before the advent of Nebuchadnezzar II, and Erech stood near the banks of the original mainstream course, now reduced to a trickle by comparison. It was a symbol perhaps of lost glory: Erech had been one of the most powerful of the ancient city-states, even before the emergence of Babylonia itself. The heart, symbolised by Venus, will sooner or later be obliged to take second place to the soul, to Jupiter.

Following this principle, all the outlying cities, towns and villages of the Mesopotamian plain were, or over the years gradually became, symbols of the physical limbs and psychological functions of a parent body, and this parent body during the first millennium BC was the city-state of Babylon. Every town had its own ruling god or goddess, and Marduk was always considered chief among these far-flung deities, no matter how much more terrible earthwards, or even how much more exalted heavenwards any of them may have seemed as individual powers.

Although these other gods and goddesses can be thought of as having a particular role to play, Marduk himself was not, and could not be, limited to any particular set of rules. The reason for this is very plain: the human soul represents wholeness; it contains all human possibilities within itself, and cannot correctly be thought of as isolated or limited in any way, or as representing this or that quality. Do not make the common mistake of assuming 'soul' to be confined to holy or spiritual matters. Marduk, as a ponderable symbol of the soul, contained every known characteristic within his own nature. This was and still is the actual nature of soul: simultaneously the nucleus and the circumference of the self, both impetus and boundary of all human actions. Even though we are not aware of it, it is only by way of soul that consciousness can reach and quicken our coarse, material parts, our sensations, emotions and thoughts. And do not make the even bigger mistake of confusing the personal soul with the holy spirit. Spirit is impersonal; soul is personal. But it is only by way of one's own soul that genuine spirituality can be contacted, that our own spiritual status can be improved, and the world of heavenly beings approached.

The Sacred Path of Marduk

Let us be onlookers at this great annual festival, for the onlookers were also thereby participants. As we assemble, the ceremony will already have begun in secret, 'invisible, beyond human sight', and known only to the Babylonian priesthood, when the idol of Marduk was ceremoniously immersed in the Euphrates – symbolically introduced to spirit and thus brought to life. Only after this initial ceremony, the act of uniting soul with spirit, had been completed, could the public procession take place.

From the banks of the great Euphrates the procession moved off with a roll of drums and a mighty clash of cymbals, a braying of horns and trumpets. Then, to the more melodious accompaniment of harps and lyres, the temple choir struck up the processional anthem of praise to the quickened Marduk. At the head of the procession walked the high priest, striking in his black and white robes, embroidered with gold. On his ornate headdress, worked in scarlet, was a winged lion, their symbol of protection from evil. Next to the priest walked his acolyte, a young lad nearing puberty, clad all in green, carrying head-high a silver bowl of holy water, freshly drawn from the Euphrates and newly blessed. Into this bowl the priest dipped a bundle of tamarisk twigs bearing leaves and flowers, and with it he sprinkled holy water left and right, from time to time arching it high in the air so that it fell as drops over the priests and dignitaries walking behind.

Immediately behind the high priest walked two ranks of lesser priests, impressive in their robes of red and black, bearing on their shoulders a woven-rush litter which swayed lightly to the rhythm of their steps. Upon the litter sat the statue, the idol of Marduk, carved out of scented cedar wood and encased in gleaming bronze, inlaid with patterns of gold, silver, and the pure blue of lapis lazuli. To the regular motion of the priests' feet,

DEEP WATERS OF SPIRIT

Marduk seemed to stir on his litter and incline his head, as though nodding and smiling to the awestruck peasants standing deferentially along each side of the stone-paved track. In his right hand, Marduk held a wooden carving: a flowering branch of the traditional tree of life. His left hand was outstretched, reaching low, the fingers bent as though holding the hand of another.

And indeed he was: only one person was allowed to hold the hand of this effigy of Marduk in public, and the watching peasants would perhaps have been all the more impressed by the figure who walked alongside the litter, reaching up and gripping Marduk's outstretched carved wooden hand. Resplendent in his ceremonial robes of purple, crimson and gold, this powerfully-built, hawk-nosed, black-bearded man was none other than the great king himself, Nebuchadnezzar II, revered restorer of Babylon after its long centuries of neglect and decay. Babylon had been great before, in the era of the world-famous Hanging Gardens, but had long since suffered through destructive politics and warfare. Now, under Nebuchadnezzar's rule, it was restored to far more even than its former glory.

The mighty Euphrates, as it rolled through the plain, had carved a niche for itself in the fertile soil, but annual flooding over thousands of years had raised its banks with layers of silt to create a series of natural levees throughout its course. Periodically these banks would burst here and there, allowing a fresh channel to leave the main stream, creating not a tributary but a branch, a minor arm of the great river itself. There were several such streams on the plain, and it was one of these secondary Euphrates rivers that approached the city of Babylon and washed its western walls. If the Euphrates represented the holy spirit, this branch of the river that approached Babylon brought to mind the age-old saw: 'Man does not approach spirit; spirit approaches man'.

After a while the procession would reach this smaller river at a point where the royal barge floated with furled sails, moored and ready, its scarlet-jacketed boatmen standing with their poles raised like guardsmen at attention. Across a broad gangway fashioned from pinewood brought from the distant Zagros mountains, the procession filed into the barge, settling Marduk's litter on a special dais amidships. With the crowd of onlookers following on the river bank, the gentle current would sweep the official party along, steadied by the boatmen's punting poles, the music of the choir and their accompaniment flushing startled ibises and herons from their cover among the willows and the reeds.

The landing stage was close by the city walls, near the beautiful Gate of Ishtar. During the brief voyage the choral singers with their harps and lyres had kept up their hymn of praise to Marduk, and to the river which bore him along, interspersed with mythical sagas set to music. But now as the processional priests again raised their burden to disembark, taking up their solemn march with the rhythmically swaying idol, the drums and wind instruments blared out again, warning the waiting citizens that the most important ceremony of their year was under way, and the procession was about to enter the city gates. They were met at the gate into the city by the mayor of Babylon, resplendent in green and gold, accompanied by his council of elders.

Their music echoed as they passed through the magnificent Ishtar Gate, one of the dazzling wonders of the newly restored Babylon, its glazed tiles and bright mosaics ablaze with blue and green and gold – mythical figures of dragons and bulls, winged lions, eagle-headed gods and lion-headed eagles, magical guardians of the city and symbols of state. The traditional paved route marking the sacred path of Marduk followed a circuitous course through the city streets, winding its way close to the walls, its length lined with townsfolk, silent and respectful. Eventually they reached the impressive temple of Marduk for the next stage of this great New Year festival.

The Arrogant, the Humble, and the Wise

The Babylonians were masters of symbolism. The great procession could take place only after a full week of preparatory ceremonies, the most important of which was known as 'the humbling of the king'. In front of the assembled council of priests and elders, the king's robes and crown were removed, and he was made to kneel before Marduk's image. At that moment the great Nebuchadnezzar (as also his father Nabopolassar before him) would have seemed no better, no more important, than any of his subjects.

The high priest then addressed the king in scathing and insulting tones, shouting unanswerable questions into his face. When he could give no answer, the priest would slap the king's face, pull his beard, twist his ears and tweak his nose until tears rolled down his cheeks. The point was being made that this person – though in fact the greatest king they had ever known, and probably genuinely respected at that – had, ritually at least, become a very ordinary creature, without pride, without benefit of wealth or privilege. This symbolic shedding of worldly riches and respect was intended to convey the message that all traces of arrogance, of self-confidence even, must be made to yield to self-doubt, to a state of helplessness similar to that at birth, if not at death, in the face of the divine will. If there could be any meaningful preparation for the forthcoming meeting with spirit, this would have to be it – acquiring humility before your own soul.

The ritual humiliation and temporary loss of power complete, the king would dress again in his robes and crown before taking part in two sacrificial procedures outside the city gates. First, within a deep trench dug in the ground, he set fire to a bundle of reeds; then he was obliged to slaughter a white bull. Remember the spiritual hierarchy extending from the ground level of materiality, through the level of plants, through the level of animals, to the original high human level lost when the Garden of Eden was lost. This was the true 'sacred path of Marduk'.

The following day another ritual was enacted: a special tabernacle was constructed, embroidered with golden thread. There the idol of Marduk was brought and set on a throne to await the visit of a subordinate but still very important god. In Babylonian mythology, this was one of his own sons: Nabu or Nebu, the god of learning and wisdom. As we already know, Nabu was the divine guardian of the neighbouring city of Borsippa on the banks of the mainstream Euphrates, and representative of the human intellect. Both Nebuchadnezzar and his father Nabopolassar had been named in his honour. When the tabernacle was ready, the image of Nabu was carried on his own cedar and rush-work litter borne by a retinue of his own priests, from his own temple in Borsippa, the ten miles or so to Babylon. The two idols were placed side by side beneath the golden surrounds of their tabernacle, in symbolic communication.

It is easy to see why these rituals were deemed essential before the main procession along the sacred path of Marduk could even take place: wisdom, or the human mind, has to acknowledge and accept the supremacy, the fatherhood of soul, before entering the spiritual life, before even taking the first step along the ultimate path. Symbolism such as this may serve to encourage the submissive attitude of faith which is the only preparation we can realistically make. The soul (represented of course by Marduk or Jupiter), having been quickened by spirit (symbolised by the waters of the Euphrates), will be carried along by that spirit and thence brought to our awareness before passing through the Ishtar Gate. Ishtar, of course, is the goddess (and the planet) we call Venus, personification of human emotions. The existence of soul has to be first accepted by the intellect, by the power of reason symbolised by Nabu or Mercury, before the inner journey can become reality. Then, sooner or later, it must be accepted by the heart, our seat of value-judgment, the means by which we can fully appreciate beauty and wonder.

The peasants on either side of the sacred path – ourselves, perhaps – are splashed by the priest's holy water, the symbol of spiritual contact coming to us by way of a flowering spray of tamarisk – the spiritual level of the plant world, and the spiritual state immediately above our solidly material, physical bodies, our brains and hearts with their thoughts and feelings. Pride and arrogance will achieve nothing in the long term; nothing can change for the better without spirit. The king must be humbled, for the only approach to spirit is by way of submission, of humility.

Understanding how nature works in essence may give us the mental flexibility to see through the solidly materiality of our lives, the materiality that holds us to the earth. The ability to see through the ungraspable but solidly material nature of water may lead us to sense the ungraspable non-materiality of spirit.

It has been said that the time for symbols is past. Today as in ancient times, without the sacred river of spirit, the symbols of religion are fated to remain lifeless idols. Without spirit having quickened the soul, the ceremonies of religion are of no more value than the superstitious trappings of idols. Whilst the soul sleeps undisturbed and unsuspected, our images of heaven will have no more reality than those precious mosaics within the beautiful Gate of Ishtar.

CHAPTER FIVE

Beasts and Birds

LIVING, SENTIENT CREATURES all vibrate with life, as we do ourselves. If we fail to discriminate between the qualities of these various vibrations, it is because our own coarse passions have become powerful enough to smother the fine-tuning device of our inner selves, allowing these things to mingle indiscriminately with our own instincts, our own vibrations of life. This is something that has already happened as a natural consequence of civilisation, and there is little to be done about it; but if we can quieten our own passions and to that extent overrule our everyday instincts, we will automatically shut out the influence of these non-human vibrations, these alien instincts, while appreciating their God-given nature.

Various kinds of meditation are recommended as a way of 'getting in touch' with our inner selves, and interesting or sometimes amazing results may well be achieved. But personal experience has convinced me that the soul itself cannot be touched or moved by these practices. 'Meditation' is not the same as 'submission'. Nevertheless it is not a bad thing to meditate quietly, allowing thoughts to be still, yet retaining an open wakeful mind. In so doing you may become aware of all manner of vibrations, all manner of essences, all kinds of nature spirits. But never forget one cardinal rule: if you aim to rise above these natural powers, to understand them and maybe even control them, make sure you remain fully conscious, and fully aware of all that goes on around you. If you cannot avoid thinking at that time, think only: 'I am human. The heavenly powers are above me, and the forces of nature are below me'. (But take this as a broad understanding, and not as some kind of mantra to be repeated, which would make nonsense of it). With this awareness, you should be influenced only by those forces which normally operate above, rather than below, the truly human level of instinctual existence.

BEASTS AND BIRDS

This is the secret of mastering these forces and understanding them: sample them, explore them, marvel at their complexity and ingenuity, but avoid being dominated by them. We should be *above* the world of nature, and not part of it. The whole of nature is completely and quite rightly dominated by the vibrations of these invisible 'lower forces', and so, quite without realising it, are the great majority of people. It is not as though they have any particular liking for nature: they may never give it a thought, but they are simply locked into the endless cycle of the natural world to such an extent that they would probably not wish to escape its clutches even if they could.

If you want to become a slave of the animals, like a character in some dreadful fairy tale, or a plaything of nature spirits; if you would like to become one with them, to be filled with them, to share their fate, to fall completely under their spell, you can. If you have ambitions to become a practising shaman or a practitioner of voodoo, you can. Simply allow yourself to fall into a trance while meditating with an open mind. Hallucinogenic drugs will serve to speed the process. You will then be influenced very powerfully by natural forces which operate on a spiritual level which is far below what should be the natural spiritual state of human beings. In your own innermost nature you will virtually have *become* an animal (or a plant, or even a material object). Once unwanted influences such as these have been acquired they are almost impossible to expel through your own will. They will carry your soul down to their level in the scheme of things. The choice is entirely an individual one, of course, but it is not a fate to be envied.

Quite a terrifying prospect, if you look at it in that way. No-one in their right mind would attempt to do such a thing voluntarily. But this sort of thing on an *unconscious* level is exactly what happens to us during our normal childhood development. The horror is a reality; the warnings have come too late. What can we do? Consider some of the frightening creatures of mythology that dreams and visions have produced, possibly to warn us of these very dangers: there is the Minotaur, half man, half bull, who lived in a labyrinth (occult realms can seem truly labyrinthine) and, like the frightful Baal Moloch, demanded human sacrifice, especially of children. He represented the highest spiritual level of the animal kingdom that really does 'swallow up' human children before they even reach the age of discretion. The story tellers and creators of myths among ancient peoples were to some extent aware of this uncontrollable descent, this impulse that carries potentially saintly humans down from their original high spiritual status to a level on a par with that of the beasts. Perhaps *everyone* knew about it at one time, but with the spread of education, with increased scientific learning, it was dismissed as nonsense.

Perhaps the most telling amongst the mythical creatures which were visualised as reflecting or symbolising the spiritual descent of humankind was Cerberus, the three-headed dog of Greek mythology, said to guard the entrance to the underworld. He had writhing snakes instead of hair, and the poisonous aconite plant (representing the next spiritual level below that of the animals) was supposed to have sprung up from the foam which dripped from his slavering jaws. He was reputed to welcome all new arrivals, fawning and wagging his tail – but once they were inside he would not allow them to leave. Again, a terrifying creature of nightmares – but so very accurate, so true. His three heads signify the three 'lower life forces', animals, plants and the material things we find so attractive – and which, once we have taken their influence in, will not let us go.

Scientifically, intellectually, of course these things are nonsense: if you analyse mythological creatures you will find nothing there. The influence of these animal life forces on the human soul may have an abstract nature, but the practical effect is very real. Even in real life, whether we seek them out or not, the wild things of nature from lions to mosquitoes sometimes thrust their possibly unwelcome presence and their influence upon us. Many centuries ago lions roamed wild in southern Europe as well as the Middle and Near East and the whole of Africa. According to the biblical Book of Proverbs, this creature was once a standard excuse for the lazy lie-abed: 'What, go outside? There may be a lion in the street!' Without trying, lions provided an ever-threatening omen for superstitiously imaginative people who tended to see signs and symbols wherever they looked.

'The great mother of the gods', Rhea in Greece, Cybele in Asia Minor, variously named elsewhere, was usually depicted in art as sharing the company of lions, which were considered sacred to her name. When she came down to earth, Cybele's chariot was supposed to be drawn along by lions. A fable (variously involving golden apples and a magical wild boar) also tells how the fleet-footed goddess Atalanta and her equally swift suitor Hippomenes, were both turned into lions by Cybele, and quite whether this was meant to be a step up or a step down in the spiritual hierarchy is not clear. Almost inevitably, Artemis or Diana was involved in this story, and she too, in her role as the 'wild wanderer' over hills and forests, representing the fearless huntress with an untamed spirit, was considered an associate of lions, and they were also considered to be one of her many symbols.

To the Babylonians, for fairly obvious reasons, the lion was a symbol of their god Nergal, 'the furious one', better known to us as the warlike Mars. Later in Europe lions were considered sacred to Dionysus, or Bacchus, to symbolise his leading role in nature as 'king of the beasts', and in the Middle East too the lion was a symbol of their nature goddess Atargatis, to represent the power – and in this case the regenerative power – of nature itself. Thus lions have variously represented danger, and the savagery of a swift predator, supernatural royalty, protective family group, faithful companions, and untrammelled freedom. The nature of the lion, it seems, will depend upon one's own nature, one's own spiritual level. Only if, like Daniel in the lion's den, you are on an inner level no lower than theirs, can you be confident in their company.

Another fierce cat, the leopard – also known as the panther

– was thought of in similar terms, again associated in Babylonian minds with their furious god Nergal. But the leopard epitomises cunning and secrecy in the forest as well as ferocity, and on this basis, even more so than the lion, was considered sacred to the often riotous, notoriously cunning, but normally secretive forest god Bacchus or Dionysus who, as soon as the grape harvest was over and the wine drunk, was reputed to haunt and hunt in all the wildest and most desolate places. The lynx too, another secretive denizen of deep forest and mountain fastness, was sacred to this same god of nature, but mainly in northern and western areas, for unlike the leopard its natural range covered most of the northern hemisphere. With its distinctive tufted ears and fabled eyesight, it was well known to the ancient British Celts who admired the lynx with a passion that transferred some of its fierce characteristics to themselves.

Predators such as lions would certainly have seemed to a community of hunter-gatherers to be top of the animal tree: not infallible perhaps as hunters, but probably proving successful more often than the human tribe who warily watched and skirted the local pride of lions. How, they wondered, could people hunt more easily, while lacking in fang and claw? It was probably this sort of question, the wish to possess something more reliable than their own bodies, to acquire the tools for the job, to be able to arrange beforehand where their next meal was coming from, it was probably this that started the downward spiritual journey towards the treasures (and perils) of the earth – and ultimately the zone of materiality – with the aim of improving their fate, and achieving mastery over nature and the earth.

Natural Magic

Desire and Magic are companions from the same stable. We have heard of the warrior who ate the lion's heart to give himself courage. This was practical 'magic' with passionate intent, and it may well have worked; there is no doubt that influences from the natural world are regularly taken in involuntarily by means of the 'passions', simply by eating our everyday food. The days when people were limited in what they ate, the simple diet of the peasant, are well on the way out. A family might have eaten nothing but rice with the occasional addition of fish; or bread with the occasional treat of beef; potatoes with the occasional slice of bacon, maize with occasional wild game; a shepherd community may have eaten only mutton or lamb. There is no doubt that whole populations were powerfully influenced by the food they ate: they took on something of the characteristics that their food had when it was still alive and growing.

It is said that you are what you eat. Sophisticated people who shop in supermarkets nowadays imbibe so wide a range of food, much of it processed and refined, that these basic influences have become well mixed and diluted. But although the characteristics of various foods and their effect on us have become well-nigh unidentifiable, the principle is still at work. Animal and plant characteristics are being distributed into the inner nature of the humans who eat them. It was through this magic process that our earliest ancestors began to acquire what I have called alien instincts. By way of their desires and through their food, their human vibrations and those of the creatures with which they came into contact became intermingled. They acquired understanding of the animals, both hunters and hunted, but in so doing their spiritual level was drawn down to equal that of the beasts themselves. The human race may well have started off in 'God's image', when their symbolic ruler in the Garden of Eden was the Father Figure, but as they were increasingly wooed by the tempting Serpent they quite rapidly became 'beasts' within their own essential nature, and with the growth of desires began to behave like intelligent beasts rather than the spiritually aloof but also vulnerably naive humans they once were.

Extroverted humans look for causes and influences outside of themselves, and as their passions became more powerful so too imagination grew, and sought to create magical means whereby their desires could be brought to reality. Spirits of nature, gods and goddesses, were visualised, and as their concept had arisen through universal human-animal instinct they were universally recognised and accepted as self-evident, though their names and the personal characteristics ascribed to them were many and varied. They fulfilled everyone's expectations. Cernunnos, the Celtic god of hunting, and similar deities in other lands, were early products of 'magic hunting'. People were hunter-gatherers before they were farmers, and of course they still loved to hunt long after they began keeping cattle and sheep. Cernunnos, already ancient, became a near-reality in Celtic hearts when hunting was no longer the only means of obtaining meat. Along with other animal-gods, he was greatly strengthened when the *passion* of hunting became a sport. Perhaps, when men had forgotten how to use their originally innate tracking skills, it seemed all the more important to call upon some kind of supernatural being to help them in the chase. This passionate god of animal life was revered by those who hunted in the forest, as an animal spirit capable of supervising their quarry's abundance and whereabouts, as well as its welfare, fertility and powers of regeneration.

Cernunnos, as the personification of animal life forces, both hunter and hunted, was pictured as an antlered figure, half man, half stag, usually sitting cross-legged among the trees. The Celts kept no written records of their beliefs and practices, but following the Roman occupations and their Latin accounts of Celtic lands, they are known to have assimilated Roman deities and combined them with their own. The feminine element of intercession took over from the ultra-masculine assertion of Cernunnos, and the Roman Diana or Artemis took the place of the antlered god. More persuasive, and perhaps that much more civilised, more likeable, it was she who became the chief Celtic hunting deity to whom sacrifices were made, and hunting tolls paid for her temple coffers.

Throughout Europe all game animals were held sacred to Artemis or Diana. Deer, above all, were strongly connected with her name; in art she has often been depicted as accompanied by deer, or riding in a chariot drawn through the forest by hinds –

female red deer. Records of ancient Greece frequently mentioned 'deer festivals', celebrations of hunting and the rudiments at least of wildlife conservation, which were held annually in her honour. They featured a feast of venison which was eaten along with cakes baked in the shape of deer. In eastern desert lands where there were no deer, the animal sacred to Astarte – their equivalent of Diana – was the gazelle. This graceful creature epitomised, and perhaps still epitomises the principle of wild nature enduring and thriving in the wilderness.

You could say, perhaps, that all animals have been associated at some time or another with one of the gods or goddesses of nature, but few have been held more in superstitious regard than the humble hare. An animal of the chase right up until the present day – obsessively so with devotees of coursing with dogs – and yet in many lands regularly associated in people's minds with the supernatural, with magic and witchcraft. In the Celtic world hares were, and perhaps in some places still are, a powerful symbol of sorcery – witches' familiars perhaps – while Scandinavians and Saxons too ascribed magical powers to this fleet-footed creature, which can unexpectedly run faster uphill than down.

In the ancient classical world, hares were considered living symbols of the satyrs, understood in the biblical prophet Isaiah's sense of 'hairy demons' which dance in the wilderness. Unlike god-demon satyrs, hares are not normally dwellers in woodland, preferring wide open spaces; but when satyrs are forced to leave their woodland surrounds (so the fables tell), perhaps because the trees have been cut down, they emerge into the open and take the form of hares, with their supernatural powers and lustful nature still intact. Always associated with the spring – perhaps because its breeding season makes it that much more conspicuous, especially when rival males dance boxing on their hind legs, the hare was linked by the Romans with their spring goddess Flora as one of her constant companions. There is certainly a sexual element in our long-standing intrigue with the hare, and the further east we go the more has it been identified with carnal desire, and for that reason intimately associated with the love-goddess Aphrodite. So familiar to country people in less sophisticated days, and still a slightly disturbing concept for us today, the hare has never been domesticated; perhaps, like Aphrodite and all she stands for, its spirit never could be tamed by men.

Nature Humbled

Hunting out of necessity has for most people long ago disappeared into the mists of folk memory, and civilisation has brought us into a strange and contradictory relationship with the wild creatures of nature. On the one hand we feel the need to protect, preserve, and conserve such wild places and their creatures as still remain; on the other hand we harbour an inbuilt mistrust, approaching a fear, even, of 'wildness', and some small part of us would like to do away with it altogether. Conservation of hunting grounds was no doubt of concern to hunter-gatherers. But even by biblical times the records show that wild creatures were thought of as something to be 'cleansed' from the land; primeval forests as something to be cleared to make way for human settlement. The concept of preserving wild places for posterity has only very recently become again a matter for concern.

Inevitably perhaps the supernatural inhabitants of the hunter-gatherer's world became carried forward and modified to encompass the lives of the earliest farmers and stock breeders. The earliest domestications seemed a magical pact between the nature gods and goddesses, men, and the beasts themselves. As one of the earliest animals to be domesticated, the goat can stand as a symbol for the domestication of animals in general, forming the first solid link between wild nature and civilisation. In its wild state the goat has always seemed closely connected with the nature gods of reproduction, of fecundity, from whom Dionysus and Bacchus later sprung. Its apparently lustful nature made sure of that. As a domestic animal it became sacred to the name of Artemis or Diana (in future, let us call her 'Diana Artemis' to make the link plain). As the favourite hunting goddess for so many hunting people, as one who understood the mind of the beast, it was only natural that she should become honorary goddess of animal-taming and stock rearing too.

As a symbol of wantonness or lust the billy goat has been pictured in art and in man's imagination as a riding animal for the sex-goddess Aphrodite, especially in her role as Pandemos, the goddess 'for all people' (a title implying that she shared the popular dislike of over-bearing morality). In ancient Rome the weird goat festivals known as the *caprotina* were held during the summer months in honour of Juno, the queen of heaven, and in art again Juno was usually depicted wearing a goatskin tunic. As goddess of marriage and the special guardian of women's rights and interests, she was thought well able to control the lustful nature of men – as symbolised by the billy goat – and this wearing of 'their skin' was intended to drive the point home.

Goats have often been associated in the popular imagination with magic, witchcraft, and the devil. The strong smell of a billy goat is said to resemble the supernatural smell of subtle materiality within the realm of the occult (a smell to make your hair stand on end). The inverted pentagram, or five-pointed star with a central point directed downwards – a symbol of black magic – is also thought to represent the front view of a billy goat's head, with the horns, ears and beard forming the five points. The capricious woodland demi-gods have been depicted as half man, half goat: half god, half devil; half spiritual, half material; supernatural creatures full of mischief, and bound to the animal nature of the earth. It was the era of the domesticated goat that brought about the birth of the great god Pan, together with his retinue of horned, goat-legged, cloven-hoofed fauns and satyrs.

As a symbol of strength, of swiftness, and above all of man's apparent mastery over nature, the horse reigns supreme. Whether in the form of giant shire horses bearing armoured knights into battle, or as sweetly gentle ponies loved by little girls, the horse has a noble ancestry and a rich mythology. Favourite of the gods, and especially sacred to the sun god Apollo or Helios, horses have always been depicted as symbolic of both supernatural and earthly power and stamina. In myth the sun rides across the sky in a gleaming chariot drawn by white horses, and Aurora, the goddess of dawn, is also carried across the morning sky in her golden chariot drawn by white horses. Even mother earth, with her various guises and numerous names, has been supposed to travel in a horse-drawn chariot, stressing the horse's connection in men's minds not only with the surface of the earth and its atmosphere, but also with the underworld itself. 'The horse rider' is one of the many titles given to the sex-goddess Aphrodite, evoking the idea of a fertility spirit in the form of a ghostly horse, said to gallop across the fields and plains by moonlight, ensuring a rich harvest for the year to come.

The goddess of horse-training to the ancient Greeks was none other than the revered Athene, the third in their heavenly triad, as though to stress just how important this skill was both to them individually and to their state. As for the Celts (who loved horses and prided themselves on their horsemanship) their goddesses Rhiannon and Epona were both strongly connected with the art of taming, training and riding horses.

Cruelty: Does it Matter?

Yes, it does! If there is one type of action that more than any other backfires on humans and fills them and their progeny with alien influences, making them act and even look like the creatures concerned, it is deliberate cruelty. A 'passion' of any kind for animals, an obsession with them, ensures an increased flow of unwanted influences; acts of deliberate cruelty towards any animal magnifies and hastens this effect. Combine 'passion' and 'cruelty' into a passion for cruelty, a passion, shall we say, for harming, roughly breaking in, enslaving, or killing whatever type of creature, high or low, ensures a veritable flood of influences, of misplaced vibrations. Unborn children are in special danger from the cruel passions of their parents: the sins of the fathers are visited upon their children, with a vengeance, and we are in a position now to see that this 'vengeance' is not a punishment, but a natural consequence.

Passions, don't forget, can include excessive love as well as hate – over-indulgent kindness, perhaps, as well as unnecessary cruelty. Pets can be a godsend for a lonely person, something on which to lavish the love and attention which would normally flow towards their family, their children, but pet-owners should be heedful. As Rudyard Kipling wrote:

Brothers and sisters I bid you beware
Of giving your heart to a dog to tear

I am sure that even Kipling himself did not realise the deeper truth hidden within his sentimental poem *The power of the dog*. But once the idea has been sown the simplest observation will confirm that this unwelcome interchange of influences has its effect on more than one level. An expectant or new father might have a passion, for example, for fishing, and purely on a physical level this passion may make itself apparent in the growing child's features. Similarly expectant or nursing parents may well have a 'thing' about flies, or mice, or goodness knows what else besides. A farming passion for cattle, for sheep, for pigs, for chickens, for horses, for camels, these passions are liable to show up in an unexpected way to blight an innocent life. The aristocratic parent's love for shooting pheasants may show up as an unwanted heirloom in their child's features, if not in their character. Most people already know this, but do not dare acknowledge it even to themselves. Perhaps the time has come to break the taboo and release the causative passions.

Misplaced love can indeed be as undesirable in this respect as hate. Too much kindness can prove as unwelcome as cruelty, because the danger lies in *passion*; a passionate relationship. Young girls often love ponies, and that is fine; but when puberty arrives it is better for them if that sense of closeness transfers itself into an interest in boyfriends. Close ties of affection develop quite naturally and strengthen into a permanent bond while the physical body is developing: horses are noble creatures with wholly moderate natures, but humans need human influence rather than horse influence. Horse-loving parents too may be putting their child's future happiness at risk. The danger time is the point at which natural vibrations, those most basic of instincts, can be picked up and introduced into a new place, a place where they have no right to be.

Domesticated animals tend to be trusting and submissive – this is the spiritual nature of animals that have, in effect, overcome their own basic instincts, when their passions have been overruled by the spiritual force immediately above their own. Given the right conditions it is a principle that can extend far beyond domestication. When applied to humans it implies the gaining of saintly status and is in tune with the flow of evolution. The principle might bring to mind Isaiah's prophetic poem:

The wolf also shall dwell with the lamb,
And the leopard shall lie down with the kid;
And the calf and the young lion and the fatling together;
And a little child shall lead them.

This quality of trusting submissiveness is in fact just the quality we need to feel in ourselves, when faced with spiritual possibilities of all kinds. Meanwhile, it pays to treat our animals with care and understanding. Most western European farmers treat their stock with care and understanding – like animals, that is, rather than humans, using reason and consideration with firmness. There will be no 'love' as such, and certainly no intentional cruelty. In this neutral, passionless way they become able to understand their animals and communicate with them as necessary, but their own inner self and the inner selves of their children will not be affected.

Animals themselves, of course, are not kind to each other,

except when their own instincts prompt them; but anyone can see that there is nothing intentional or wilful in this – they are behaving in their own natural way. A wild creature has to eat, and the concept of humane killing will not be understood. In the human sphere there are whole races of mankind who are akin to the world of animals at the level of their souls, and they sometimes seem to treat their animals with what may appear to westerners to be quite appalling cruelty. But these people do not see it that way: they are simply following their innate nature. No particular passion is usually involved, so the worst effects of misplaced vibrations will not arise for them. These are people who were created and who still live within 'the realm of the serpent'. It may seem strange, but the concept of being 'kind to dumb animals' belongs to people who have descended within the spiritual hierarchy to the level of materiality – the realm of Satan himself! An enigma indeed, and one which will explain itself in due course.

Eagle's Wings

Heraldic lions can readily turn into heraldic eagles by way of the gryphon. The ability of birds to soar into the heavens has to that extent set them on a pedestal – it has made them at least seem to occupy a higher niche in the spiritual order of things than the earthbound beasts. For our earliest ancestors who still lived almost exclusively within the truly human spiritual level, artefacts of all kinds, tools, weapons, even clothes, were non-existent and unimaginable – until they took the plunge, overruling their own submissive instincts to begin the wilful descent. By way of the animal and plant worlds, they gradually began to attain more and more of the material benefits of the earth as their inventive capacity grew, at the cost it seems of their original status above the beasts. To primitive humans, birds were probably no more than birds, and the power of flight little more than a means of escape from predators. The mythical Daedalus and Icarus made their wings not to ascend to heaven, but merely to escape from the prison island. It was not until the human spiritual descent had reached the inner level of the plants, and sunk below the status even of birds, that people began to imagine individual souls and angels as possessing wings. They were looking *up* at the spiritual level above their own.

Like the gigantic roc, only the powerful but wholly impersonal life forces that envelop the earth were thought of and symbolised as having wings, of having the capacity to seize and transport whom they will between heaven and earth. The fabulous gryphon, half lion, half eagle, was the instinctively invoked symbol of power with a spiritual element, both on earth and in the sky. This was the invisible life force said to guard the treasures of the earth: the impulse which led early man to look downwards, to see the answer to his problems in the acquisition of worldly wealth, to trust his progress to and through the lower life forces by way of the world of beasts. Human life without the benefit of material wealth was fairly meaningless, and from the time of the first written records, from the time of the prophet Abraham, men were not looking towards the world of angels to carry them forward or to being the benefits of civilisation: their progress inevitably took them on a downward spiritual path.

Everything that has been said about animals regarding unwanted 'influences' applies in equal measure to the birds, and their distinctive natures and features also have been shared extensively and invasively by unsuspecting people. Having mentioned the unfortunate consequences of over-enthusiastic pheasant shooting, the same could be said about birds of prey and those such as gamekeepers whose passion it may have been to control their numbers. Perhaps Moses had this outcome in mind when he formulated his list of proscribed birds and beasts – the list sometimes known as the Mosaic dietary laws. A sensitive eye such as his would have noticed the effects making their appearance among his followers during their forty years of wandering in the desert. Those ancient Hebrews of course were not interested in game conservation and the concomitant killing of predatory and egg-eating birds. They were nomads, and as they often went hungry they would have been quite passionate about obtaining food; if they could catch a bird or bring one down with their slings, their desire would be to eat it, whatever the former lifestyle of the bird.

At all events, Moses painstakingly listed all the flesh, fish and carrion-eating birds they encountered (selecting from the various translations available): eagle, falcon, hawk, kite, osprey, lammergeier or ossifrage, night hawk, desert owl, fisher owl, great owl, horned owl, little owl, long-eared owl, short-eared owl, screech owl, tawny owl, bearded vulture, black vulture, Egyptian vulture, gier vulture, griffon vulture, scavengers such as the raven and the crow, also the cormorant and its ilk, the heron, the stork, the pelican, and for good measure the cuckoo (which many have mistaken for a hawk), the hoopoe and the swan.

Since the far-off days of Moses, birds have found a place in the world's mythology. Even then hawks and falcons, in the Egypt which Moses and his people had fled, were symbols of the sky-god Horus, connected through their tenacity and mobility with the principle of annual regrowth in due season, and the idea of rebirth. Inevitably, during the centuries intervening, the eagle has been considered a sacred symbol; to the Romans, symbolic of Jove or Jupiter; to the Greeks, of Zeus, and to both of them and to numerous other lesser nations, a symbol of the sun god Apollo or Helios. The eagle's fearlessness and mastery of flight, allowing it to soar high over the earth while observing everything that was happening on the ground below, ensured its eminent, almost supernatural status. But to the people of northern lands, and to Vikings or Norsemen in particular, the eagle was given a different connotation: to them it implied doom and gloom, savage indifference to suffering, and the approach of wild, stormy weather. Equated with their own ideals, the eagle made its appearance mirrored in the rapacious habits and sharp features of the fierce invaders who explored their northern world by sea and in so doing plagued the more peace-loving people of the lands round about.

For who knows how many millennia, birds have been regarded as omens foretelling events. This is hardly surprising for, being free to fly around at will, they are always liable to put in an appearance, whether predictably or unexpectedly, fortuitously or ominously. Forget about the unfair and quite modern slur of 'harbingers of death' that have bedevilled a few, such as the exquisitely beautiful barn owl: see it instead as the alluring symbol of Minerva, Roman goddess of wisdom and culture. Or the magnificent raven: instead of a sinister bird of ill-omen see it as the impressive symbol of Apollo, especially when sunlight reflects from its gleaming black plumage; a symbol too of the supreme northern god Odin or Woden; or, if you prefer, an aerial companion to the queen of heaven, the Roman Juno or the Greek Hera, divine patroness of women's rights. Or the handsome crow: instead of an omen of contention and strife, see it too as a symbol of Apollo, the sheen of its plumage reflecting sunlight in glossy green; another symbol also of the queen of heaven. There is nobility in these birds that is not to be decried: a pedigree that extends back in time to the age of the dinosaurs.

In fact, birds can augur whatever you wish, and if you look in places where they are likely to be found, perhaps you can make your prophecies come true: when your omen appears, it means you will have found what you are looking for. Much of the mythology of birds is plain to understand: the joyful sound of the cuckoo has gladdened people's hearts since seasons began, and small wonder that it has played a part in so many tales as the herald of spring. Similarly with the obvious grace and beauty of the swan; the apparent gentleness and purity of the dove; the proud finery of the peacock; the clarion wake-up call of the rooster.

You can take the romantic view, typified by the Greek myth of the nightingale: Aedon, a bereaved mother, was bewailing the death of her son when Zeus heard her; disturbed by her bitter lament, he turned her into a nightingale so that she could lament more sweetly through the night. Its song is certainly heart-achingly beautiful. The dipper sings in the tumult of its mountain stream, its song modelled on the tinkling sound of running water over pebbles. Birds never make meaningless sounds: their voices are

BEASTS AND BIRDS

full of awareness, from the wistful chirping of the solitary budgie in its cage, longing for an answer, to the African boubou shrike which, concealed in the bush, stages a finely timed duet between male and female. Or you can take the practical approach. An excellent way to keep alert to nature, to stay tuned, is to learn the notes and songs of all the birds common to your area, to learn their language, so that their conversation is always in your ears. Like some people, birds tend to project their feelings and voice their concerns, and this means they can tell you a great deal about the local environment and its wildlife which you may not see for yourself.

CHAPTER SIX

Insect Dharma

THE NAME OF BAAL-ZEBUB, also known as Beelzebub, the original Lord of the Flies, demon-god of pre-Israelite Palestine, conjures up a dire image of blood-soaked places where animal and perhaps human sacrifices were made, a place where flies would have abounded, feeding freely and breeding rapidly. It recalls the belief once widely held that insects generate spontaneously from decaying vegetation or flesh, for these flies, as though created by Baal, would seem to have emerged from the sacrificial rites themselves. Traditionally, flies have seemed to carry a kind of mystery, an association with the supernatural. Those kinds which naturally seek the light, often seeming to materialise out of thin air, were thought an expression of the local Baal and tolerated unquestioningly. Those kinds which naturally seek out caverns and dark places, however – the blowflies, flesh-flies, greenbottles, and bluebottles or blue-tailed flies, with their shining metallic colours moving freely from the sunlight into darkness and back again – were assumed to have a connection with the underworld. During the classical age of Rome and Greece, as living go-betweens attending the rites of Pluto, Persephone, Attis and other gods and goddesses of winter, death, and reappearance in spring, flesh-flies were considered to be special wards of the enchantress Circe and her patroness Hecate, feared moon-goddess of witchcraft and magic.

'Dharma', a Sanskrit word, is taken to mean living according to one's own God-given nature. This, as a rule, is what insects do; it is people who tend to fall short in this respect; we are only human. But one thing to be avoided if at all possible is to find oneself filled with the dharma of insects – a fairly common fate. The insect kingdom with its myriad lifestyles is full of wonders on what seems to us to be a miniature scale; it is filled with breathtaking beauty, again on a miniature scale, as well as scarcely believable horrors. Many people of course see only unpleasant creepy-crawlies which they would rather not have to see at all. Others become captivated by the sheer beauty and amazing inventiveness of the insect world. We can all appreciate the beauty of a butterfly's wing; not so many see charm in other insects, those which buzz and crawl and bite and run and burrow. There are many people (and often quite pleasant people too) who would rather crush a fly than bother to open a window and let it fly away.

This insect kingdom is where the vibrations of nature are most obvious, nearest the surface, speeding up very noticeably under the influence of the sun. Our appreciation of these creatures which together form so large a slice of creation is admirable, in my view, but the unseen danger creeps in with them. When simple pleasure turns to addiction, or equally when distaste turns into disgust, when wholesome appreciation develops into scientific study, when economic entomology, insect damage, pest control, preventative measures, or even forensic entomology, experiments in insect breeding and genetics, collecting and killing, whether for its own sake or with a scientific end in sight – when these things become a passion, these are the periods of greatest danger. Because the 'vibrations' of these creatures are so close to the surface, acts of cruelty towards insects (however they may be phrased) are fraught with spiritual peril. I am not claiming that insects actually *mind* when you are being cruel to them: I simply don't know whether they do or not. Shakespeare obviously thought they did, according to the words he put into Isabella's mouth in *Measure for Measure:*

> *And the poor beetle, that we tread upon,*
> *In corporal sufferance finds a pang as great*
> *As when a giant dies.*

Certain people whose religion prompts them to believe in reincarnation scrupulously avoid doing harm to insects when they can – not, if the truth be told, out of concern for the insect's welfare, as lesser creatures on the ladder of life, but because such people have been made aware that their own future spiritual welfare may well be harmed through their careless actions. So many people in the world today (especially, perhaps, devoutly religious people) tend to see only the chaos of variety in the world, rather than an immense and intricately woven pattern, a tapestry of connected life forms, each creature filling its own interrelated niche, its own square inch of beautifully designed embroidery. So many people see the world of nature as disconnected, fragmented and unpredictable, as unrelated creations scattered over the earth: a grasshopper here, a rain shower there; a sparrow here, a drought there; a cactus here, a kangaroo there. This may be the standard pre-scientific world view, but it is still alive and flourishing in the minds even of intelligent, well-educated folk as well as the naive peasantry of the world.

It is not a primitive view. To the over-civilised the concept of nature as an integrated whole can seem totally alien and scarcely comprehensible. This kind of fragmentation of the perception of nature presents a threat to the spiritual integrity of the individual. People like this may have 'done science' or studied biology in school; they may even *be* scientists of one sort or another themselves. It may happen that, like a person from a pre-scientific cultural background who goes to college and studies a scientific subject, appreciation of nature's integrity can be bypassed. In one great step we can move from not caring at all, to the point of obsession. Passions are readily aroused and easily misplaced.

Even today, with all the 'green' propaganda and the wonderful wildlife documentaries on TV which allow us all to observe at the closest of quarters the intimate lives of even the rarest of creatures, certain media people who should know better still seem to treat the whole subject as a sort of no-man's land. Even now, the papers will 'say anything'. Things are improving, of course. 'Insect knowledge' was an utterly alien concept before the 18th century, as far as records show. Only a few years back any individual who actually knew one kind of bug from another was mocked as a hopeless eccentric. Me, I am on old Lady Glanville's side. Do you recall the name? Perhaps she started it; she was certainly one of the pioneers: the drive towards making entomology a respectable and respected pursuit. Then again, perhaps she merely exemplified the western European's propensity to become hexed by the insect soul. England is said to be the land of eccentrics, and it is from there that we can best look back to discover the eccentric truth.

It was thought perfectly in order to guess, but not to actually observe insect lives. The first great English naturalist is said to have been John Ray (1627–1705). His first interest was botany, which by then through its association with herbalism was considered an almost respectable subject, but he switched to entomology under the patronage of the remarkable Lady Glanville (she is remembered particularly in the name of a butterfly – the Glanville Fritillary, a species that reaches the northern extreme of its range at the southern English coast, and at the time of writing is just barely hanging on in the Isle of Wight). When the good lady died, her will was contested by some of her family on the grounds of insanity, as plainly evidenced by her apparent obsession with insects. John Ray went to court to give evidence on her behalf, successfully, as it turned out. He represented the voice of educated reason by demonstrating scientific order and God-given beauty in a field of study where most people could see only confusion and chaotic diversity of form.

The Teeming Rhythm of Life

Non-human creatures listen to one another because their ears are attuned. Your dog hears the birds in the garden speak of a cat, and runs outside to look. Insects can communicate too, especially when the many act as one; their lives are full of warnings and premonitions. If you visit some place where insects really abound, such as tropical bush country, it is easy to feel the rhythm of all these individual characters acting *en masse*. In the long grass they tell you plainly enough when some person or sizeable creature is on the move. In unison, their songs will change or stop. Flies home in on the intruder. Butterflies rise in a cloud. Grasshoppers leap out of the way, their bodies arcing high through the air before diving head first into safe cover. Soldier ants rear up and open their jaws at the vibration of a footstep. Ticks clinging to the grass stems open their little arms at every rustle, to embrace whatever creature comes their way. The attackers: warble flies, bot flies, horse flies, tsetse flies, thirsty for blood, zoom in with manoeuvrability and speed, watching with proboscis-daggers drawn for the chance to stab and drink.

Insects may be less obvious in temperate lands, but they still abound. You may decide to pick a few heads of cow-parsley to add to your flower arrangement and bring them home, only to find that you have introduced a dozen or more different species of insect into your house. The great *users* of insects (and all wildlife) are the tribal people of tropical lands. They know what to use and what to swat and what to ignore. Any romance or poetic appreciation that there might have been with regard to insect life becomes bogged down with practical questions: can you eat it? Can you squash it and smear it on? Can you wear it? This is one way of seeing order and design in the great plan, one way of staying attuned. Appreciating order and design in the scientific sense is something else, and in between the two are the lost millions and the faded centuries which have seen only baffling variety and lack of appreciation.

The matter-of-fact approach born of over-familiarity means that you don't get many ethnic poets writing about insects. They simply don't get emotional about them. The subject would seem far too basic, too banal for poetry. But English poets have often been so moved, particularly the madder ones. Peasant poet John Clare (1793–1864) is my favourite. He *felt* for insects in a way quite foreign to his times, which is probably one reason why he ended his days in a mental asylum. He was so moved by the false hope aroused in the insect world by an unseasonably warm February day, that he wrote:

INSECT DHARMA

'Neath hedge and walls that screen the wind,
The gnats for play will flock together;
And e'en poor flies some hope will find
To venture in the mocking weather;
From out their hiding-holes again,
With feeble pace, they often creep
Along the sun-warmed window-pane
Like dreaming things that walk in sleep.

Whilst poor John was spending his final years in the asylum, he wrote of the ladybird bug (called the 'clock-a-clay' in his local dialect) lying hidden in the cowslip pip while the uncaring world went on around it, as though he had actually become that unconsidered creature, hidden from the eyes of passers-by and as unheeded as he was himself. Certainly few of his contemporaries deigned to notice the world that teemed beneath their feet and above their heads.

Here I live, lone clock-a-clay,
Watching for the time of day.

Perhaps John Clare began by merely *noticing* that tiny creatures like the glossy red black-spotted ladybirds have God-given beauty, and that their little lives have enormous purpose. He would have watched the winter gnats dancing, rising and falling in unison, thinning and thickening, drifting like smoke – intriguingly so, perhaps, against the hazy background of a leafless larch wood. Are they one soul in unison, or many? Unlike the shoaling of fish and the flocking of birds, the winter gnats' swarming instinct is based not on self-preservation, but rather the urge to mate. Every now and then a pair of gnats will meet up, and drop together out of the dancing throng.

Throughout the insect world the urge to mate is greater than the individual instinct of self-preservation. I daresay you, like I, have seen a stag beetle trying to copulate with his mate, several days after she has been well and truly squashed into the tarmac by a passing car. Death and reproduction, death and sex are closely allied in the insect saga; endings and beginnings are contiguous within their life cycle. An insect sliced in two will often react by trying to carry on copulating with its copulating half, whilst carrying on eating with its eating half. Death is ever-present, and sex is ever-rampant. Look at the interactive social ceremonies of the fierce carabid beetles, extruding their enormous curved *penes* glistening like burnished brass.

What an incredibly beautiful, frightening world is the world of insects! As the docile browsers and grazers among them go about their peaceful affairs, green and crimson parasitic wasps like tiny scourges roam each branch, waving flashing scimitars, searching for newly-hatched caterpillars, straddling them, caressing them, probing them to find the softest baby flesh in which to cradle their own golden children. Eat, little ones! But leave the vital organs till last, or your food supply will run out!

Spiders are far more obvious in their predatory ways, but never call them insects. Spiders look down with tolerance on their cousins the ticks and mites, and look up with respect to their fiercer cousins the scorpions. Spiders too can flaunt surreal beauty, especially perhaps the jewel-like thorn spiders of the watery, ferny tropical forests, sitting like Christmas tree decorations in the centre of their webs above cool streams, their 'thorns' like stars rayed pink and green. As a rule, the largest spiders are the more harmless; the enormous slow-moving hairy ones are quite docile. The man-eaters as a rule are smaller and thinner and far less noticeable. Tarantulas are almost cuddly by comparison. You may sometimes get the impression that spiders lord it over the insects whilst appreciating their beauty too. If you think this far-fetched, stretch the imagination a little and look at the neatly silk-wrapped butterflies offered by certain spiders as courting gifts. But the tables can be turned in favour of the insects, when they get the chance. The larder-nest of the solitary wasp is well stocked with hunched rows of spiders, alive but paralysed, each cradling a soft white wasp egg balanced on its hairy belly.

Parasites of the Soul

William Blake (1747–1827) of *Jerusalem* fame, could be described as *the* metaphysical insect man, though perhaps he didn't realise the connection himself. But he was well aware of the pernicious ways by which alien beings can invade the soul. In his *Auguries of Innocence* he warns us that:

> *He who torments the Chafer's Sprite*
> *Weaves a bower of endless night.*

Obscure it may be, but it is very telling in our present context. And of course, better known and perhaps better understood, there is:

> *The caterpillar on the leaf*
> *Repeats to thee thy mother's grief.*
> *Kill not the moth nor butterfly,*
> *For the last judgement draweth nigh.*

For Blake, the last judgement was an individual matter for each one of us to face at death. According to him, 'all deities reside in the human breast', so how much more were the strange ghostly visions which he recorded also part of his own being. He was in the habit of sitting up into the small hours with his friend, the artist-astrologer and ghost hunter John Varley, both hoping to capture on paper the essence of these strange larvae when they put in an appearance. It is not simply by coincidence that the prior meaning of 'larva' is 'ghost'.

I recall in particular his own pencil drawing of 'the spectral flea', one of the ghosts which, so he claimed, emerged from his own self. His flea-self showed cruel animal teeth and an eager serpent tongue 'whisking in and out of his mouth, a cup in his hand to hold blood, and covered with a scaly skin of gold and green', all drawn with great attention to detail. It was of course a self-portrait of Blake, in *one aspect* of his personality. He really did behave rather like a flea, tramping restlessly round at all hours, drawing out his own particular brand of nourishment, his insatiable thirst for the unknown, ever hungry for his own inner content, never afraid to parasitise his friends for theirs.

Larva-art is to be found in high places, too. In the English post-war Coventry cathedral, for instance, where Graham Sutherland's 75 foot high *Christ in Glory* might perhaps have been better named *Christ in Chrysalis*, the figure half emerged from a cocoon of tumbled white silk, shot through with muted insect colours of crimson and purple against a leafy green background. The same famous artist was said to keep bees trapped in his window so that he could study them close at hand as they buzzed endlessly up and down the pane, as though drinking in their desire to fly free.

Bees all too readily swarm into their beekeeper. If bee-watching has its perils, some of the more obsessive bee enthusiasts are almost frighteningly bee-like. They probably will not sting; they are peaceful enough creatures, but they really have no need to feed on royal jelly while humming quietly to themselves, or sprout dark bristles on their skinny wrists like a *Tales of the unexpected* character by Roald Dahl, before the metamorphosis becomes permanent. Don't forget that bees and their honey were for many centuries thought to be specially favoured by the goddess of witchcraft, Hecate, and sacrifices of honey were made in her honour. Remember furthermore that the Greek god of beekeepers was the rampant penis-god Priapus, who took command after the god of fair weather, Aristaeus, had provided favourable conditions. Between them they indulged the demi-goddess Melissa, sweet personification of honey itself. Sex and the supernatural so often go hand in hand.

Be assured that the 'Roald Dahl effect' results from 'passion' rather than the simple enjoyment of a honey sandwich. But it has been said before and will no doubt be said again: you are what you eat. Ravenous swarms of locusts can descend out of the blue and ruin whole farming communities in a few minutes, and an attack can devastate the peasant economy. But locusts do have one redeeming feature in that you can eat them: and of course this is what happens; the victims of locust attack make the best of a bad job. But look around the world: people who eat locusts do tend, like the locusts themselves, to destroy every sparse morsel of vegetation in their neighbourhood. These are the lands where the very last bushy shrub is wrenched out of the ground to feed the cooking fire.

No doubt you can find further examples if you look for them. Certain tribal people who like to eat caterpillars – particularly the enormous, sluggish ones, certainly do tend to become sedentary pastoralists, without very much to show in the way of aggression or very strong a defence mechanism. Some kinds of termites are favoured as food in some places, particularly the large amber queens, sweet and fatty-tasting, which emerge from the ground when the first rains arrive, and obligingly unhook and discard their wings as a prelude to mating. You may find that such people, like the termites themselves, prefer to live crowded together in communal huts. Not so with jackals, which sit for hours by the nest-hole scoffing termites as they emerge. They are solitary creatures, but *their* hunger, their daily sustenance, is not a 'passion'.

Bush fires send insects scattering, and a grass fire in any tropical land will attract birds, beasts and humans, all stuffing scorched bugs into their mouths. The big plant bugs lightly scorched (don't let them stick their deadly spears into your thumb, they don't wholly appreciate being eaten) taste strongly of almonds; the large grasshoppers have a nutty taste; all a good source of protein. We can all appreciate the important part some insects play in the life of the countryside, whether they are food themselves or not. Gravedigger beetles purify the land by burying the scraps missed by scavengers, conferring the last rites on the tiny corpses of birds and mice hidden among the grass stems and beneath the leaves. The equally hard-working scarab dung beetles play their part on the African plains by rolling away and burying neat balls of animal dung. Amazing creatures these; the ancient Egyptians looked on the scarab with superstitious awe, and it featured in their hieroglyphic system.

The real-life magician Aleister Crowley thought highly of magic scarabs, though he usually kept clear of insects when he and his followers practised magical sacrifices. They certainly imbibed some kinds of influences from their sacrificial victims, but Crowley was well aware of the dangers involved. On the subject of magical sacrifice, and comparing a small victim like an insect with something like a bull, he wrote:

The amount of energy disengaged at the sacrifice is almost unimaginably great, and out of all proportion to the strength of the animal. Consequently, the magician may easily be overwhelmed and obsessed by the force which he has let loose; it will then manifest itself in its lowest and most objectionable form.

Magical and religious sacrifices take place in many lands, of course, of animals, birds, and (probably even now) of humans. But *every* deliberately contrived death is a sacrifice, in the sense of every creature finding its destiny. The victim, though never consulted, is confidently supposed through its sacrifice to find its highest purpose in the spiritual sense. Even in the insect world the food chain should involve an upward spiral, for the victim in each case is or should be used by the spiritual force immediately above it: minerals by plants, plants by animals, animals by humans, humans by angels... Could it be that unpalatable creatures never rise to their true destiny? Like disagreeable people, will they stew forever in their own juice?

Mythology based on the dharma of insects, and the strange interchange of contents between the human psyche (and even the human body) and the teeming, vibrating forces of nature, probably started out as true stories. To illustrate the point, here is a ready-made true story:

INSECT DHARMA

When I had to visit an indigenous forest reserve deep in the Kalahari-sand area of southern Africa, I was given the low-down on the local forester. "You'll like Skinny Jameson", they said. "He's quite a character". Oh yes, I thought: Skinny, eh? He's probably a big fat chap. But no; the nickname was cruelly accurate. His large frame was painfully thin. Even his African nickname translated as 'bones'.

Skinny had been born and brought up in these parts, so it really was home to him. For normal day-to-day business, the clickety local language was his first tongue. He knew how to walk fast and far in soft sand – the 'Kalahari crawl'; how to keep yourself from getting dehydrated; how to keep meat eatable without a fridge in the 100° shade temperature. He was a perfect example of the right man in the right job, and he loved the forest, sparse as it was, and everything in it. Yes, I got on well with him from the first. His face and build looked somehow familiar, almost as though I had seen him before, though I was sure I had not.

You only get to know somebody properly after the barrier of reserve has broken itself down and you no longer have to be polite. This can happen more quickly in the bush than in the town. A few mornings later we were watching some toktokkie beetles demonstrating how they got their popular name, and how they communicate, sending sexy drum messages to each other by 'toktokking' their rumps on the ground wherever they found an area of sand that was hard or compacted enough to act as a sounding board. Their rhythmic tapping carries some distance.

Skinny chuckled. "Toktokkie farm!" he said. "When I was a nipper I used to make toktokkie farms. I used to fence all the toktokkies together in little kraals. Then I'd forget about them and the poor things would starve to death". I suddenly realised why as a stranger he had looked familiar. With his gaunt frame and pleasant-funny beetle face, he *was* a giant human toktokkie, perpetually on the point of starvation, hollow as death.

Having a scientific interest in insects does not really help. Professional entomologists might be thought immune to this sort of thing, but not a bit of it! They are easily identified. One would hardly go in for that sort of job unless one had a certain passion for the little beasts, and entomologists tend to specialise. Perhaps coleopterists – the ones who specialise in beetles – are the easiest to spot; like Skinny Jameson they exude the essence of beetle in their face, their figure and their bearing.

Don't scoff. It can happen to you. I once knew a man who lived in the middle of a forest in a little log cabin. He was plagued by cockroaches that hid away in the wooden walls, so much so that he took to creeping about at night with a lighted candle, inflicting fire torture on the ones unlucky enough to be caught. Collectively though, the insects had the last laugh, as usual. The poor chap became more and more cockroach-like until he could hardly bear to emerge into the daylight, preferring to scuttle out of his hidey-hole only at dusk. But he was a caring soul. Cockroaches are great parents, dragging their little silken baby bouncers full of offspring, wherever they go. In fact, he was the nicest chap you could wish to meet – if only you could ever get close enough to speak to him.

CHAPTER SEVEN

The Plant Kingdom

AS THOUGH POISED midway between heaven and hell, the Green Man, symbolic ruler of the plant kingdom and the people who live on that spiritual plane, is a god-demon. He is a wholly masculine concept: there is no 'Green Woman'. He bridges the gap between the old gods and goddesses of forest and field, and the era of religious thought based on a more truly spiritual understanding – as distinct from merely a religious set of beliefs. Behind the old disjointed way of seeing nature as a random collection of beings and seasonal phenomena, is the acknowledgment of a general and continuing life cycle: coming into being, flourishing, fruiting, dying down and disappearing, only to be reborn again and again.

This was old-style 'integration' – the ancient understanding which unquestioningly accepted a kind of reproduction or rebirth into the same situation as before, the same status for people on earth, repeated over and over. World religions brought hope of rebirth into a higher condition, a higher spiritual life form, offering a chance to leave behind the repetitive cycle of nature. The Green Man links these two understandings. Forest guardian he may be, as he represents the plant life force of the earth, but in concept he relates solely to human welfare; unlike Pan or Faunus he is not concerned with flocks, herds or crops.

Matching the history of human development in microcosm, one's individual spiritual progress from birth onwards involves a downward trip, from babyhood into progressively thicker layers of materiality and the adulthood of civilisation. When this learning process, this imbibing of materiality, is complete – the end of a one-way journey to the very gates of the underworld – the old gods and goddesses of nature will have done their job. It is then that the great religions of the world appear, explaining by way of symbols something of spiritual truth, at a time in human development when a way back up the spiritual ladder is possible and can be indicated. The way has to involve a climb through the plant kingdom, through the kingdom of animals, finally to reach the human point of birth – now the point of rebirth – where it is possible in the Christian terminology to 'become again like a little child'. The underworld with all its attractions will then have been left behind, and further progress should be in a heavenwards direction.

The Green Man stands at the gateway of this great divide between on the one hand the kingdoms of humans, animals and plants, on the other the alluring world of materiality. Like Janus, the two-faced Roman god of doorways, he guards this gate and looks both ways at once. To a young, developing, descending soul he holds the key to materiality: treasures, power, luxury, magic, and the illusory paradise sought by so many. In this role he looks like a god, but is really a demon, for the territory above which he stands and whose gate he guards is the realm of Satan himself. To the matured soul having reached the lowest gate and seeking at last to ascend and by atonement escape the endless cycle of natural becoming, he threatens the loss of wealth, comfort and security, indicating only the wild and scarcely trodden forest path. In this role he looks like a demon but is really a god, for he stands, as it were, on the first rung of the ladder to heaven. In this role he is the highest and most enduring of all gods and goddesses of nature. As though in instinctive acknowledgment of this unique position, the Green Man's image appears in many a Christian church, carved into wood or stone: a strong human face wreathed in leaves, often with vegetation growing out of his mouth; a seemingly lowly forest deity, but to the people who placed him there a way-keeper to heaven itself.

There are whole races of mankind who, at the level of the passions that habitually fill the developing, descending soul, bear an uncannily close relationship with the plant kingdom. Though they may seem to us to act in slow motion, plants in their own instincts are ruthless, and aggressively competitive – they have to be in order to survive the pitiless cut-and-thrust of their natural world. But when looked at from a higher spiritual level – or should I say from a higher level of the passions that exist at soul level – plants seem peaceful; and patient. This too is the nature of people who by their birth and ancestry seem to be in some way racially aligned with the plant kingdom. And like the Green Man who has no female counterpart, they tend to exalt the masculine and subdue or conceal the feminine element amongst themselves. They even tend to treat each other as though they were real plants, occasionally pruning and lopping those whom they wish to curtail.

When plants are being eaten by animals or humans, their highest nature is being realised, their destiny fulfilled, and instead of resisting fiercely they are patiently compliant and submissive. People who have this close relationship with plants too can be very patient, tolerating equably even the most difficult of living conditions. But when their passions are stirred on their own lowest level, or when incited by a spiritual level beneath their own, rather than some sort of higher destiny they will see only exploitation, oppression, threats and hardship. At such times these people will seem arrogant and uncontrollably aggressive. They adopt the instincts that should rightfully belong to the plants themselves. Strangely enough, these 'plant people' tend to live in places, such as desert lands, where real plant life is very sparse indeed. It is almost as though the life forces that should be clothing the ground with vegetation are flowing instead into the people, being taken up and absorbed by the human population.

'Plant people' in their religious beliefs are, collectively at least, aware of the satanic nature of the life forces beneath them, and though fascinated by the thought of the wealth and luxury to be found in this spiritual zone of materiality, are usually persuaded to remain where they are, dithering over the abyss. It is not really their conscious intent, of course. And though they sense rightly that the world they affect to despise is indeed the realm of Satan, they cannot help but envy those other races which have taken the plunge. Because of the fierce nature of human-plant instincts, from all the material benefits available they tend to select some of the more destructive 'benefits', such as weapons of war, for themselves.

Taming the Wildwood

People who live in forest land as their natural habitat, and find their livelihood there, are unlikely to be 'plant-soul' people. They are much more likely to be 'animal-soul' people, or even 'material-soul' people. Forest dwellers are fewer in numbers nowadays than once was the case. Forests all over the world have for so many centuries been cleared for cultivation and, rightly or wrongly, are still being cleared at a rapidly accelerating pace today. The people doing the clearing would no doubt claim that they are actively working towards the further development of civilisation.

In materially orientated societies, soul differences are becoming more and more diluted and less readily to be identified. But elsewhere in the world (shall we say, in the Third World), if people are deliberately 'cruel' to plants in the sense that they are wilfully destroying the forest, or even recklessly disposing of individual plants without attempting to make proper use of them, either for their own purposes or as food or shelter for their animals, the vibrations of plant instinct may well enter their inner selves. It is much the same, if less obvious, as when animal instincts (and most noticeably insect instincts) take up residence within people who direct their passions towards them – particularly if such people have had deliberate destruction in mind.

This is not the same as 'plant people' who live in desert lands. It is not a matter of race, of being ancestrally allied to these natural orders of animals and plants, and to that extent sharing their qualities; no, it is merely part of the normal decline in spiritual values of the human race, a gradual growing-away from the original high human status – the natural descent through successive layers of instinct, with a spiritual centre of gravity corresponding first with animals, then with plants, finally with things – keeping pace all the way with the development of modern civilisation. So there are three causes of plant instincts affecting human behaviour: the first is a racial or ancestral compatibility with the characteristics of plants at the collective level of the passions and desires which prompt most of our actions; the second is purely individual and depends upon the reckless application of those passions; the third is one's normal development from childhood to adulthood, one's soul level passing through the instinctual influence of the plant kingdom, in common with the rest of the human race.

If they can look back far enough into their own history, most races of the world will recognise a mythological hero-figure said to have taught the earliest farmers how to cultivate crops, and how to grow trees and fruit. To the Egyptians the first agricultural instructor of the peasantry was Osiris; to the Greeks he was Eumolphos (a handsome green butterfly has been named after him, and what better way could there be to commemorate the origins of tree-planting). Both these mythical figures (and numerous others) have been credited too with introducing the cultivation of grape vines and the production of wine. This must be one of the most ancient of agricultural enterprises. After all, the biblical Book of Genesis tells how Noah's first priority after his ark grounded was to plant vines. He drank all too heartily of his produce, and caused a drunken incident which brought enduring problems for his second son, Ham, and his Hamitic descendants.

Drinking wine, indeed, increases the passions and (or so it seems at the time) enhances them. As the gods and goddesses of classical times were personifications of human passions, pains and pleasures, it follows that the deities associated with wine and the vine are numerous. Eumolphus came to be considered the first god of vines; the divine overseer Jupiter watched over the vintage as closely as he watched over everything else; so did Rhea, the all-important mother of the gods. The germination and fertilisation of vine plants was down to Priapus, also Bacchus or Dionysus who looked forward to drinking the finished product. Aristaeus, the fair weather god, protected the growing vines, defended them against excessive summer heat, and protected the swelling grapes from drying out. Libitina presided over vineyards; the god-demon of harvest Agatho-daemon also presided over vineyards, and if displeased could visit disaster in the form of blight on the swelling grapes. Pan too was closely involved; Liber and his consort Libera guarded the wine as it was fermenting, and no doubt drank freely of it; Persephone as representative of autumn vegetation was also considered a goddess of wine.

Vine leaves were associated with Bacchus Dionysus (let us link the two names as they are both representative of the same mythological character) and also the Roman goddess Bona Dea. The wineskin itself was a symbol of Silenus, the drunken attendant of Bacchus Dionysus. A favourite subject in art, Silenus has always been depicted as a fat little old man being supported by fauns and satyrs, or riding and often falling off a donkey as he swigged from his wineskin. Great wine festivals have been held in all vine-growing lands, but of course the history and mythology of ancient Greece and Rome are chiefly the ones which have been handed down to us. All these lands have had their equivalents of the *vinalia* when Jupiter, Venus, Hermes and Bacchus Dionysus were honoured as all the human participants got gloriously drunk. The same applied to the *dionysia* and *bacchanalia* festivals dedicated to Bacchus Dionysus alone, where central to the festivities a wooden statue of the god was set up and wreathed in vine leaves. Because ivy leaves bore some resemblance to vine leaves, if the vine leaves had all fallen when the festival was held, evergreen ivy leaves were traditionally used instead.

Getting drunk is, in fact, a quick and most effective way of imbibing 'plant essence', experiencing its nature and storing it up within your own being. Not only wine but, I suppose, every alcoholic drink has been brewed or distilled from plant material, representing what amounts to concentrated plant essence on the material level. As we have seen, a 'plant person' has, on the one extreme, patience; on the other extreme, fury. A person under the influence of drink, we might say, has on the one extreme, an inclination towards reckless or aggressive disorderly behaviour; on the other extreme, the total patience of unconsciousness.

Above all this, however, grapes were also eaten both fresh and dried as a welcome food, along with all the other fruits and berries. The cultivation of orchards and groves of fruit trees began, naturally enough, with the gathering of wild fruit and berries. The date palm and fig tree feature in the most ancient of literature, and almost inevitably various deities have been associated with them in men's minds. They readily lend themselves to symbolism. Date palms are 'sunny' trees, there is no doubt about it, and they have often been depicted in art as a symbol of the sun god Apollo or Helios. Fig trees on the other hand are more typical of light woodland, of potential pasturelands, giving shade to the earliest domesticated herds of cattle. Their fallen figs are eaten avidly by grazing and browsing animals, and they soon acquired the reputation of helping breeding cows to calve safely and give plentiful milk. For this reason perhaps they were thought especially sacred to Ruminus and Rumina, the god and goddess respectively of suckling calves. The fabled 'fig tree of Rumina' was the tree beneath which the twin founders of Rome, Romulus and Remus, were supposed to have been suckled by their surrogate mother the she-wolf.

The Romans had a nickname for the men who chopped trees down: 'woodpeckers', and when the earliest cultivation of orchard trees and plantations began, cutting down the existing trees was of course a necessary prelude. To supervise this operation they invented the woodpecker god, Picus. I like to think of the European red-capped green woodpecker, *Picus pluvius viridis*, – 'Picus, the green rainbird' – in this role. The first innovative use of fertiliser in the form of animal dung, and its application to the ground, was also attributed to Picus. Even today in some peasant lands, animal dung is used primarily as fuel for the cooking fires rather than manure for the land, and these people probably have little choice. But when a certain degree of soil degradation has been reached, when desert conditions set in, it is notoriously difficult to raise the standards again. When it became clear that plants benefit so greatly from an annual application of dung, orchard cultivation and especially agriculture took a great leap forward. We can imagine the bird-god Picus leaving the forest edge to pick the grubs out of the scattered manure, before calling upon the rain (which he is supposed able to do) to wash it into the ground and reach the hungry roots.

Perhaps when cultivated varieties of olive trees began to arrive in ancient Italy, the newly discovered principle of fertilising the fields and orchards received a setback, for it was soon discovered that, like the wild olives found throughout the Middle East and along the northern shores of the Mediterranean, these trees thrive on poor, dry, stony soil, and do less well, bear poorer crops, and suffer from more ailments when grown on rich sites. Perhaps this is why they had been the earliest-known orchard crop to be grown in the poor, dry, stony soil typical of Greece. Of all crops the Greeks most prized their olives, eaten fresh or pickled, and when improved varieties made the production of olive oil a major commercial enterprise they valued them even more. Perhaps it was the idea of pouring oil on troubled waters, and the evergreen olive tree's capacity to flourish on the poorest hilly sites, which suggested the qualities of peace and wisdom and associated the olive in their minds with Irene, the goddess of peace, as well as Minerva, the goddess of wisdom. In the name of their chief goddess, Pallas Athene, at the new year olive branches were carried in procession to honour Helios, god of the sun, and speed his return to strength in the spring.

The Romans probably found apple tree orchards easier to establish successfully, and they conjured up a new goddess, Pomona, to look after the health of the growing trees and the quality of the crop. Her symbol was the pruning knife, and it was supposed that her best work was done in the winter and during blossom time. Her consort was said to be Vertumnos, already well established as the god responsible for the change of seasons, whose touch made the leaves turn colour and fall to the ground. Pomona having tended the trees through the year and ensured a good crop of developing fruit, Vertumnus protected the ripening apples, ensuring that the fruit swelled evenly and coloured attractively.

Anyone having the use of a piece of land is often inclined to cultivate a garden, and this will reflect the needs, likes and dislikes of the owner. Inevitably, perhaps, most gardens of the ancient world – like most Third World gardens today – were practical places where vegetables and small scale food crops were grown. But gradually, with an improvement in economic conditions, flower gardens cultivated for pleasure rather than necessity came into being. Some deities were closely involved in this, and they were invariably the most 'beautiful' ones. 'Goddess of gardens' was one of the titles given to Aphrodite, and in ancient Greece (and in her birth-place Cyprus) many flower gardens were made and maintained in her honour. Similarly in Rome, ornamental gardens which included flowers and herbs were considered the special province of Venus. The handsome Adonis too was closely associated with gardens, the cultivation of flowers and fragrant herbs. At his festivals in areas which fell under the Grecian influence extensive displays of flowering plants were laid out on display, all the local women, it is said, vying with each other to produce the most beautiful miniature container gardens. In Roman areas the *floralia* festivals were held in honour of Flora, the goddess of spring, of flowers, and humans in the bloom of youth – particularly beautiful maidens. Women would wear colourful floral dresses, and the men and their working animals would be decked with flowers, especially the goddess's favourite roses.

In classical days it is plain that there had to be a motive behind growing and displaying flowers; it seems there was precious little enjoyment of flowers in their own right, for the next millennium or more. Plants that were not of direct practical use were taken as symbols: of unseen powers, of supernatural beauty, of hopes and fears, of life and death. Most flowers featuring in the stories of mythology have a connection with death, usually followed by rebirth in one form or another. Several are supposed to have sprung from the blood of a slain god-hero: anemones, from the blood of Adonis killed by a wild boar in the forest; hyacinths, from the blood of Hyacinthus killed accidentally during a tiff between Apollo and Zephyrus; violets, from the blood of Attis with his self-inflicted wound beneath the pine tree. And then there was the narcissus which sprang up on the river bank, after the vain youth of that name leaped into the water in amorous pursuit of his own reflection. If you want a posy to symbolise the underworld in mythological terms, choose narcissus and asphodel, set off by the greenery of maidenhair fern and cypress foliage, both said to grow at the entrance to Hades: not at all gloomy, by the way, and a very tasteful arrangement.

Herbal folklore no doubt flourished in ancient times, with medicinal herbs, pot herbs, herbs for every superstitious precaution, for as Rudyard Kipling noted:

Anything green that grew out of the mould
Was an excellent herb to our fathers of old.

In addition to their obvious practical uses, herbs were also used as symbols (and indeed, some of them are still so used to the present day – rosemary for remembrance, rue for repentance). Some plants played a dual role: myrtle was a firm favourite, a popular medicine and a source of incense, considered sacred to Aphrodite and Venus (who was sometimes called Myrtea, the myrtle goddess), to Demeter, Persephone, and to Myrrha, the mother of Adonis. Marjoram, origanum, dittany, fragrant and attractive in appearance, herbs such as these were held sacred to the name of Diana Artemis, besides their inclusion in the gardens tended in honour of the handsome vegetation-god Adonis.

A British art dealer told me recently that the most popular paintings (or, at least, the ones he was most likely to sell) were studies of poppies. It is not merely their bright colour (most people in the west associate poppies with brilliant red); they carry with them a rather romantic image of harvest time, of idyllic sunny days in the country. And of course in classical times poppies were equally highly regarded, and held sacred to the name of Ceres, the corn goddess, to Demeter, the mother-goddess of vegetation, to Agatho-daemon, guardian spirit of the cornfields, and, further east, to Aphrodite, representing the principle of fruitful femininity. But somewhere along the line poppies have acquired a somewhat dubious reputation as the source of opiates.

Narcotic drugs produced from plants of course have valuable medicinal uses. But for some people they act as a lure, promising a glimpse of a 'plant paradise' waiting to be experienced. And indeed they can bring this about: but it might occur to you that the sensations, the elation and the analgesia induced by narcotics are by nature the 'passions' of a plant that is being eaten or used by an animal or a human. They represent, as it were, the plant's highest destiny. An addicted person may reach a state of mind where material resources are seen only as a means of procuring and intensifying these sensations. Like a fly caught in a Venus's fly-trap, the human victim will have become trapped within the subtle quasi-supernatural world of the plant kingdom.

Say it with Flowers

Nowadays the great majority of people appreciate flowers for their own beauty, and an attractive flower arrangement in the home certainly will have an emotional effect on the people who live in the house, and it may well impress visitors too. This is its practical effect; but the Zen-based art of ikebana flower arranging is more symbolic than practical. Its aim is to point you towards the inner dimension, whilst still giving you full rein to enjoy the natural beauty of cut flowers. There are several different branches, or specialisations, or schools within this ancient Japanese art, and if you wish to take it up seriously as a skill or pursue it as a hobby you will certainly be learning about these different ways and trying out all the variations. But at heart, in its basics, ikebana is simple enough: it encourages you to express your feelings and explore your own inner state in a quiet way that will make you feel more peaceful, more patient – the highest 'passion' that can be expressed on the level of the spiritual plant life forces. You really can 'say it with flowers'. If you work at it quietly, your own inner self will take a hand and guide you in a way that may amaze you. The essence of ikebana, then, is not so much to make a pleasant flower arrangement that others will admire, as to reflect upon and quieten your own state of mind; it offers you a way to approach your own inner feelings, and gives you an awareness of inner peace.

Before starting, make sure your mind is calm and relaxed; forget any worries you may have. One of the delights of ikebana is that you can get away with using very few and very simple materials – there is no need to buy bunches of expensive flowers. Select your material with great care however, it has to mean something to you. Almost anything of a suitable size that pleases your eye may be used – a branch, even a piece of dead wood, leaves, berries, grass, can all be valuable. A flowering spray from a tree or shrub often forms the best possible base to start from.

Having assembled your simple ingredients, let their own nature decide the nature of your finished arrangement; don't try to force them. Whichever school of ikebana you follow, the basic principle will be the same: the celestial triad, or *seika*, is expressed as *shin* (heaven), *soe* (humanity), and *hikae* (earth). Any supporting material you may wish to use around the base of your arrangement is called *jushi*. Ikebana arrangements usually have a front and a back: there will be the aspect facing the observer, and this is called 'south', symbolically facing the sun and blossoming in full light; there will of course be two sides and a 'north', partly hidden from view, perhaps, part-shaded, and rather more barren than the south. Looked at from the 'western' side *shin* will be highest, arching to the right. Below this will be *soe,* below this again, *hikae*.

Work on the principle that 'a little is good'; the simpler the arrangement, within reason, the better or more satisfying the results should be. The plant material representing 'Heaven' will be high-arching, leaning slightly perhaps towards the viewer. 'Humanity' will be massed centrally, representing the people living on earth within the confines of nature. 'Earth', complete with its treasures, perhaps, will be lower and wider-spreading, and any supporting material you decide to use will be arranged around the base to balance your design. The principle could of course be applied as well to larger arrangements with a more generous supply of flowers. But at all events it is something to be done carefully, calmly, trying to feel the essence of your arrangement that is taking shape. Following your intuition, something very satisfying is sure to develop from it.

Listen to the Trees

Everybody has heard of 'hugging a tree'. Listening to the trees, like listening to good music, can 'soothe the savage breast'. Quietly contemplating a mature tree, or merely experiencing the proximity of trees, or breathing in the peaceful atmosphere of a forest grove, particularly if you are able to empty or relax your mind, will bring a sense of calm. And yet the knowledge which we have gained, our overall view of the plant power-struggle constantly being waged, tells us that the inner nature of a tree, its natural instincts, urge it to be aggressively fierce, selfishly ruthless, determined to win at all costs. These seem to be conflicting extremes. How can this seeming contradiction be explained?

The previous chapter touched upon the food chain – life forms in general tend to be eaten by the occupants of the next higher spiritual level, and thereby reach their own highest destiny. Actually, the victim is not being 'eaten' in spiritual terms, but rather being 'used' by a higher life form. This is what you are doing: using the tree, and thus ensuring that its higher spiritual as opposed to its passionate or instinctive nature is to the fore. The tree's instinct may be to struggle and kill for its own place on earth, but its spiritual nature is to be patient, trusting and submissive. When you metaphorically 'hug a tree', not only are you nurturing the tree's own higher nature, you are acquiring true patience for yourself – a deep feeling of peace.

It is an observable fact that a mature tree growing and thriving will have found a certain balance, its own balance within nature, which enables it to live in harmony with the rest of creation. This is the feeling you are picking up – reconciliation, atonement, an attitude that enables you to live with an inner peace, even when surrounded by hubbub or unpleasantness, or even danger. It means you are accepting life as it is, with all its ups and downs, and learning to live in harmony not only with your fellows, but with your own self.

Trees 'used' in this sense can offer a way up, as it were, through layers of natural instinct. But a tree needs to be well established, and well on its way to maturity, before you can make use of it in this way; you are unlikely to obtain the same feeling of peace if you allow yourself to be filled with the 'spiritual nature' of tree seedlings or saplings still trying to find their own place in the sun. At this level, young trees are very insecure and their instincts are vigorous and savage (whether they themselves have conscious awareness or not), and can project a sense of apprehension which you may pick up. They have not yet found their own peace: their world is full of strife, and the threat of battles to come; you will find no calmness there.

There are so many notable trees in the world that have not been included in this short list, like the giant redwoods of California, the eucalypts of Australia, the teaks and mahoganies to be found in tropical lands, and numerous other noble trees, because it would be impossible (and probably not very helpful) to attempt to evaluate them all. Be practical about it: if you find a certain tree impressive and accessible, approach it, listen to it, and feel its peaceful presence if you can – it may well pay dividends. At all events the experience will bring you that much closer to understanding something of the instinctual force governing the world of plants, and their highest 'passion' – the passion of patience.

THE PLANT KINGDOM

ALDER A very distinctive tree that loves the waterside, and is thus very valuable in shielding cool water from the sun, and keeping it fresh; a tree of myth and legend in the Celtic world where it is known as *gwernen*. The name *gwern,* an alder grove, often appears on modern maps in places where there are now no trees, recalling the march of time, and the development of land as well as the gradually changing climate. The Romans made good use of the alder, which they called *alnus,* a name which they often used also to mean a small wooden boat, for which the rich red-brown timber was ideal. The wood was used traditionally to make wooden clogs until quite recently. As a tree to contemplate quietly, it bestows a sense of peace overriding chaotic emotions.

ASH The ash tree has a special place even today in the hearts of Norse people, who once revered the mythical *yggdrasil,* the giant ash tree that was supposed to link heaven, earth and hell; all northern ash trees reflect some fraction of its glory. The ash was known as *fraxinus* to the Romans, who found its smoothly flexible timber ideally suited for fashioning their chariots and carts. The Celts also greatly valued this tree, which they called *onn* – not for the sake of its timber, for they preferred the tough inflexibility of the oak – but for what they saw as its fairy-like properties. The ash-grove – *llwyn onn* in modern Welsh – has druidic significance and features in myths, songs and stories of past grandeur and devotion. With its ashen-grey bark, smooth when young and picturesquely fissured with age, its dainty summer foliage, its stout black winter buds, and its winged seeds which often hang in bunches on the bare branches in winter, this is an impressive tree, notably tolerant of smaller plants growing around its feet.

BEECH In ancient times both the Greeks and the Romans knew the beech, calling it *fagus*. Its smooth grey bark remains smooth even in very old trees, and few are more majestic in their old age. Few trees too are more assertive in their occupation of forest land, dominating their neighbours. When young they are able to grow in the shade beneath other trees, forcing their way through the leaf canopy; then they branch out, spreading their own heavy shade over the top of the competing species, suppressing them, and finally killing them and taking over their space. So heavy is their shade that nothing can survive for long beneath mature beech trees, except for a few fungi and mosses which enjoy the dark. As a forest tree, like the oak, beech widens its range slowly; beechmast nuts, like acorns, are heavy and will not roll far. Forest creatures, squirrels and jays, accelerate the process by carrying the nuts away and burying them as a winter store, and when they fail to return a new beech tree grows. This is the quality embodied by the spirit of the beech: to use what means it can to engage and overcome the opposition; to win the struggle or die in the attempt.

BIRCH Graceful white lady of the forest, well known mainly in the northern lands and mountainous regions of Europe, Asia and North America. The Romans knew this graceful tree in the foothills of the Alps, and called it *betula*, a name derived from the Celtic name *betw* or *bedw* – still the Welsh name for the birch tree today. Through its silver-white bark it has been associated with the moon and moonlight, and has been held sacred to the names of several northern goddesses associated with the moon. The birch grove, *betws*, has druidic significance, and nowadays is the Welsh name for a chapel or meeting place. A tree of unparalleled beauty, quickly grown and short-lived, quick to spread into new areas as a 'pioneer species', a good 'nurse' for other young trees which are able to flourish beneath its light shade, in its turn quickly overgrown by larger trees, the birch tree is truly expressive of fleeting grace.

CEDAR The cedar of Lebanon is the famous timber tree imported by the biblical King Solomon for the building of his temple and palaces, beautiful sweet-scented wood which has been valued by craftsmen for many centuries. Amongst her many other responsibilities, Diana Artemis was once honoured as Cedreatis, 'the cedar goddess', by growers of trees, woodcutters, carpenters, and all who used the fragrant cedar wood in their work. Stately and magnificent, associated with the stately grounds of mansions and palaces, few trees could be more historical and more beautiful. The

North African Atlas cedar, and the Indian Deodar cedar, are also magnificent trees, better suited than the cedar of Lebanon for growing in small gardens. The Atlas cedar has a very popular glaucous-blue variety which is the one usually seen in cultivation. As for the much-admired *Cedrus libani* itself, it is truly the aristocrat of trees, proud and majestic: these are the qualities which seem to emanate from mature cedars. They are trees to be revered from all points of view.

CHERRY One of the first trees of the forest to come into bloom in the spring, quickly followed by brightly coloured young leaves, eventually producing the succulent fruit loved equally by birds and humans. It was one of the first trees, too, to have been cultivated in orchards, and the woodpecker god Picus is thought to have a special affection for the cherry. Among the most attractive of trees – even in winter with its beautifully marked and brightly coloured bark to catch the eye – the cherry seems to epitomise unspoilt, bountiful nature.

CHESTNUT The so-called Spanish or sweet chestnut, a native of the Mediterranean region, has been cultivated for its nuts ever since the first cultivations began. It was introduced into Britain by the Romans who planted it near their villas. They knew it as *castanea*, and surviving native Celts such as the present day Welsh, know it as *castan* to this day. Rather similar species are to be found in China and Japan, and in North America. Roasted chestnuts are a firm favourite in all countries which support the tree, though the best nuts for eating grow in warmer climes. The timber it produces is often coppiced or cut over to produce straight poles, which can be cleft into narrow pales useful for fences. Few trees are more majestic when grown to their full dimensions, with their large and distinctively serrated leaves and quite amazingly ridged, roughly spiral bark. An avenue of chestnuts bestows an air of dignity and pride to its home ground. To sit quietly on a bench beneath these beautiful trees is to imbibe something of their quality of peaceful confidence.

ELM In Europe, including Britain, and in the united States and Canada, elms have been devastated by Dutch elm disease (so-called because it was first identified by the Dutch and not because the infected trees are Dutch). Fortunately, young growth is not affected by the fungus until it reaches three metres or more in height, and the tree suckers readily; a large proportion of English hedgerows are composed of healthy young elms. This means that elms as a whole are able to survive an outbreak, and will surely recover fully in time. It is not the first occasion for this disaster to happen: analysis of fossilised pollen taken from bogs and lakes shows that elms abounded in ancient times. Then suddenly they disappeared for a century or so, eventually to reappear and repeat the process. A great pity of course, because elms are magnificent trees, and in the past their towering shapes were completely typical at least of the British countryside. Their spirit lives on, and we can be sure that they will return in strength one day for some future generation to enjoy.

FIR To the Romans the fir tree was *abies*, the name of the genus we know today as the silver firs. In the category of 'firs' we can also include the North American Douglas fir, and the spruces – in particular the European Norway spruce and the North American Sitka spruce – all of which thrive in Europe and make magnificent trees when grown in the situations and in the type of soil they find most agreeable. They all exude the pleasant smell of resin – tree huggers will get it on their clothes – and an undoubted air of majesty. Douglas fir, one of the tallest trees in Britain, and the silver firs in particular can project the sentiment of pride and power in the most peaceful sense of the words. Norway spruce is perhaps more modest in its apparent character, though still a magnificent tree. But conifers of this type, with their tall straight stems and comparatively short branches, tend to lack the calm serenity of mature hardwood or broadleaved trees, whose spreading branches can reach out as though to return your embrace.

HAWTHORN The May tree, one of the favourite small trees of northern Europe, and the origin of the traditional maypole. Few trees have been more closely associated with superstitious practices, as well as the innocent celebration of spring, than has the May tree with its annually welcome blossom. In some years during the month of May almost every British farm hedge is white with its blossoms, and the portent then for the rest of the year is said to be good. Small, thorny, and ruggedly picturesque, the hawthorn is certainly an attractive little tree, particularly useful to wildlife when its berries ripen to dark red in late summer and autumn. Eminently suitable for laying or layering to form a most effective animal-barrier hedge, in this form it provides protection for small birds and mammals throughout the year. To revere the hawthorn is to acknowledge the excellent principle of living with nature without damaging it.

HAZEL   A tiny tree, very picturesque, and well known for its attractive catkins, to be followed by the valuable nuts in late summer. Inevitably it has been one of the most useful of trees to the people of by-gone ages, for when cut back and coppiced it produces excellent rods and poles for a multitude of uses. The British Celts called it *cyll,* or *collen,* and the Romans called it *corylus.* Cutting back prolongs the life of the hazel, and if you find an apparently old, gnarled specimen, it is probably one that has avoided being cut back. Most people treat the hazel with something akin to quiet affection, and this is the mood that you should pick up when you are at peace in a hazel grove.

HORSE CHESTNUT   Known to the ancient Greeks as *hippocastanum,* the name 'horse' (*hippo*) in this sense can imply a coarse variety of something, such as a 'horse mushroom' suitable only for animals. The conkers – horse chestnuts – are really 'coarse chestnuts'. But there is another connection with horses, for when one of the large palmate leaves falls off, it displays a scar shaped like a horseshoe, complete with its nails. Our imagination might suppose that the subtle vibrations left behind by numerous generations of children (and adults) who have enjoyed playing games with the friendly-looking conkers may perhaps in some way have been imbibed by the tree and remembered in spirit. The spikes of pink or white flowers in the spring are beautiful, both individually and *en masse*. Tall and handsome, this tree will spread its own brand of happiness among those who value it quietly.

LARCH Most coniferous trees, being evergreen, have been taken at one time or another to symbolise immortality; but the larch is a deciduous conifer, very beautiful in the spring when the pale green soft-needle leaves are unfurling, handsome in full leaf, and strangely attractive in winter, when the coloured stems and twigs seen from a distance adopt the hazy appearance of smoke. The ground beneath larch groves is always well covered with vegetation, summer and winter. This is a friendly tree which seems to enjoy company.

LIME One of the symbols of the goddess Aphrodite or Venus, known to the Romans as *tilia*, and a magnificent tree for planting in town streets. Tall and rugged, hardy yet with delicate beauty in the spring when the pale green leaves are emerging from their pink sheaths; soon after, it becomes covered with small scented creamy flowers, alive with bees. In the autumn the leaves turn a clear yellow before falling very early, as though eager to rest for the winter. A tree which seems to bring a welcome breath of idyllic countryside into city streets.

OAK In many cultures the oak is considered the most important tree of the forest, and the Romans, who called it *quercus*, valued it for its impressive appearance and steadfast qualities. They considered the individual tree sacred to Jupiter (symbolic of the human soul), while groves of oak were held sacred to Diana Artemis. Oak leaf garlands were presented to Roman citizens who had shown outstanding bravery. They called the timber *robur*, meaning stout-hearted or robust, and *Quercus robur* is the botanical name for the lowland or English oak to this day. The Celts held the oak in the highest esteem, and the sacred groves of the druids were of oak, which they called *derwen*; the druids themselves were called *derwydd* – the oak people. Mistletoe which grew on oak was thought to be specially important, and played a

THE PLANT KINGDOM

major part in the druids' magical ceremonies. The Anglo-Saxons and the Norsemen considered the oak sacred to Thor, the god of thunder. In more gentle vein, all over Europe in particular, oaks have been thought of as inhabited by friendly woodland nymphs called dryads, or hamadryads. More superstitious respect has been paid to the oak than to any other tree. Historically, individual oak trees have been associated with several famous people over the centuries: King Charles II hid in an oak after his defeat at the battle of Worcester; Owen Glyndwr sat in an oak to watch the battle of Shrewsbury; William the Conqueror is said to have sheltered from a storm under an oak. Boughs of English oak were used to build the wooden ships of Nelson's navy. It is just possible that one or two oaks planted before the last Roman settlers left the British shores are still thriving today, so long-lived are they. Many other oaks in many other lands also have their long histories and specialised uses: the cork oak, the evergreen holm oak, the scarlet oak; there are of course several American oaks each with its own individuality. In fact, so many qualities and inbuilt memories are associated with oaks, that these magnificent trees deserve to be looked upon with reverence.

PINE In many countries of the world pines seem to fit a category midway between the firs and the broadleaf trees. In advanced maturity they acquire a calm but rugged serenity, with their spreading crowns and gnarled branches. The Scots pine, native to Europe including Britain, is particularly beautiful when growing in an open situation. As it matures it adopts a sturdy, weather-beaten appearance, and the flaky orange bark on its upper stems and branches provide a striking contrast with the bright green of its needles. Like the firs, pines have a pleasant, resinous perfume. As stately evergreen trees, it is easy to see why pines in the ancient world were considered sacred to Attis, the god of vegetation which dies down over winter to grow again in spring; sacred too to Rhea, or Cybele, both called 'mother of the gods', and the pine cone in particular was a special symbol of Pan and Dionysus. In short, the pine symbolises immortality within the cycle of nature, and this enduringly noble quality is the peaceful influence to be experienced by its human admirers.

PLANE There are many hybrid varieties of the magnificent trees the Romans called *platanus*. The North American buttonwood is a member of the genus, and the London plane is best known to the British, although it thrives in numerous other countries by numerous other names as well. Though by nature perhaps it would be most at home on the banks of a river or in moist woodland, the London plane is one of the most accommodating trees around, greatly admired for its ability to thrive in city conditions. Its wonderfully ornamental bark flaking into a patchwork pattern has much to do with its ability to withstand grime, for the outer bark is renewed annually before it can become clogged. The result is a perpetually clean, young-looking tree, and its fresh appearance is enhanced by the bright green maple-like leaves and ornamental dangling-ball seed cases. In town the plane is normally lopped regularly to keep the spread of its crown in check, but even so few trees are more stately or shapely. This is a tree to be admired from all points of view; it exudes good health, hardiness, vigour, adaptability, and resilience to conditions that would quickly overcome most other trees.

ROWAN Also known as mountain ash, the name given to this tree by the Romans was *aucuparia*, a purely practical name which meant 'bird catcher'. Its plentiful supply of bright red berries which ripen in late summer and autumn attract large numbers of birds, especially starlings, conveniently for commercial bird catchers who would smear the branches with sticky 'bird lime'. An old English name for the rowan is the witchen tree, for few trees have been held in such superstitious regard over the centuries. The twigs and branches are said to ward off evil and witches' curses, and crosses made of rowan wood used to be set up over the doorways of houses and cowsheds, or burnt on purifying fires. Growing happily and often isolated in the toughest and most exposed of sites, as well as sheltered gardens, the rowan expresses the qualities of resistance, determination, and the prolific fruition of nature.

WALNUT The Anglo-Saxons named this tree walnut, which means 'foreign nut'. The Roman scholar Pliny called it 'Jupiter's acorn', or *Jovis glans*, and derived from this Latin name we get the

THE PLANT KINGDOM

botanical generic name in use today: *Juglans*, With its smooth grey and somewhat beech-like bark and its large dark green leaves it is a handsome tree, and its timber has for centuries been highly valued for its beautiful grain and colour, especially when used for high-class furniture. The mature tree often takes on a weather-beaten, gnarled appearance in northern climes – slightly coarse outwardly, perhaps, but gifted inwardly, we could say, with hidden properties of excellence. The popular nut inside its tough shell bears a remarkable similarity to a miniature human brain, and perhaps because of this the walnut has been thought to possess oracular powers. Certainly the nuts are rich in vitamin E, known to be good for the brain. Contemplating this tree may not bestow particularly penetrating powers of reasoning, but it should being a sense of friendship and quiet enjoyment.

Contemplating trees – in public at least – may seem to some a slightly eccentric pursuit, but there is another, less conspicuous way. A tried and true method of meditating in the company of a mature tree is to go in for bonsai – the ancient Japanese art of cultivating artificially dwarfed trees in shallow containers. They are real trees, with all the character of their full-sized brethren. On the face of it, the life of these tiny trees may be thought a hard one, partially starved and brutally curtailed, forced to live within the very restricted compass of a small bowl; and yet they flourish – provided, of course, that they are properly looked after. Bonsai are not indoor plants: they are true trees, and as such need an outdoor environment, only being brought into the house occasionally and for short periods. Like most other living things trees respond to 'tender loving care'. They may be dwarfed, but their maturity has been achieved within what seems to them a secure and peaceful environment. There is no competition for them; they have all they need for life. By their instincts trees may seem selfish and greedy, but they are not gluttons when there is no longer any need for them to grab what they can.

Bonsai trees have been relieved of the struggle of nature, and live, shall we say, the life of a miniature lapdog, cosseted and fed on choice morsels by its loving mistress – as opposed perhaps to a wild dog which is obliged to hunt and scavenge for its living. The dog itself probably does not realise that it has been reduced to a dwarf-like stature and robbed in some way of its wild inheritance. It does not worry over its imagined loss; it knows only that life is good. Similarly, a properly grown bonsai tree cannot know that it has been miniaturised and is being cultivated purely for the pleasure of its owner. On the contrary, it has reached its highest destiny, having been delivered from the perils of existence in the wild forest. Serious Japanese growers of bonsai value this aspect of their art most of all: the inner supernatural dimension, centred around contemplation, leading on perhaps to meaningful meditation, leading in turn to spiritual submission. The coming to maturity of a tree, large or small, can certainly help instil in us the quality of patience, and this could prove the turning-point in our journey of the soul.

CHAPTER EIGHT

The Cycle of Nature

THE CYCLE OF NATURE is the life of the planet, the essence of the great world dream: a process of continuity based on the universal triad. You may call this triad 'action, reaction and outcome', or 'channel, vessel and new creation', or 'yesterday, today and tomorrow', or 'the caterpillar, the chrysalis and the butterfly', or 'seed, growth and harvest', or 'death, metamorphosis and rebirth'. Failure of the cycle to recur in any aspect, or an interruption at any point, is liable to spell disaster, not only for nature, but for human life too. The cycle is less apparent to those whose harvest is limited to a weekly expedition to the supermarket; very obvious to those who live close to the soil. Their awareness of the importance of this recurrent triad is based on experience, on expectation, on caution, on hope, all tempered with faith. To be on the safe side and keep the wheels oiled, faith in the continuing cycle is interspersed with a little propitiation of the spirits of nature.

Thinking about these things did not arise in the Garden of Eden; it was not within the province of the hunter-gatherer; it all started with agriculture. The Teutonic people regarded the principle of agriculture as basically male, involved in fertilising mother earth, so it became personified as a father-figure. To the Scandinavians the agricultural deity was Odin; to the Anglo-Saxons, Woden. The Greeks preferred to recognise agriculture as part and parcel of the mother-earth principle, and paid homage to the goddess Demeter, also to Pallas Athene; in Crete especially agriculture was thought to have been presided over by Rhea, mother of the gods. In ancient Rome reverence was given to the goddess Ceres, though perhaps the chief goddess of agriculture was once again the earth mother herself – Acca Larentia, or Dea Dia. Ancient Egyptians preferred to recognise both male and female aspects, and venerated the goddess Isis (cow-goddess of the River

Nile) and the god Osiris as joint agricultural deities, Isis to look after the annual flood, Osiris to produce the crops. Babylonians too depended on their river – the Euphrates, and to a lesser extent on the Tigris – on their mother earth, Atargatis, and the cooperation and goodwill of their freshwater god Enki.

Inextricably bound up with agriculture and thus with the cycle of nature itself, was the subject of fertility. Of all the gods and goddesses connected with the fertility of the land, those represented by the planets reigned supreme. Amongst them was to be found Mars or Ares, whose divine guardianship of the vernal equinox ushered in spring with its fresh growth and new birth. Farmers are fairly pragmatic people as a rule, and whichever god or goddess they called upon, even the queen of heaven herself, whichever name they invoked in the hope of transferring some heavenly qualities to their land, to bless their herds and pastures, it was really no more than 'hope'. Heavenly beings might bestow the benefits of mild spring weather, and the right mix of sunshine and showers to ensure healthy crops. The earth-gods Pan, Bacchus Dionysus, and Priapus – the personification of sex – assisted by still lesser divine beings, nymphs and fauns, would, they hoped, put these blessings into practical application on their farmlands by providing day to day care for the plants and beasts. But more important, more helpful to their cause than all these deities, was the break-through discovery of the use of fertiliser – the beneficial practice of spreading animal dung on the land.

The cycle of nature as it has affected ordinary people over the years by way of the cycle of agriculture, became centred on one subject of near religious significance: corn, the general term for grain crops. More than anything else it symbolised the welfare, the standard of living, the wealth and happiness of the people. Whilst alive and growing in the ground, it seemed to possess almost supernatural importance, connected with the underworld. Then came the harvesters with their sickles, watched over by the gods of the sky; and after cutting, the corn left the agricultural sphere and came under the wholly practical auspices of Mercury or Hermes,

THE CYCLE OF NATURE

the god of commerce. The lives and livelihoods of the great majority of people once depended (and in many places still depend) upon the success or failure of the annual grain harvest. The unpredictability of it all was quite understandably tied up with ancient beliefs in even more ancient unseen powers.

Different aspects of the crop, its cultivation and final yield, have been ascribed to a great diversity of deities. In ancient Canaan the corn god was Dagon, to whom sacrifices were prudently made in the hope of a good harvest. Throughout Europe and much of Asia too, supplications were made to the powers of the earth, to Hades or Pluto, and to mother earth herself, under any of her numerous names and guises. Sun, moon and planets, and all the many gods and goddesses associated with the weather as it applied to the welfare of growing plants, would be involved or invoked at harvest time, and held accountable for its success or failure. Above all, in this context, the sun god Apollo or Helios uniquely possessed the ability to supply the correct balance of sunshine and showers favourable for all crops, whether grain or grapes. Perhaps the most practical god of the harvest was, to the Romans, Saturnus; to the Greeks, Kronos, in either case the old man with the sickle.

But the feminine element of intercession was thought essential in most cultures. Chief among the goddesses of the harvest were, for the Greeks, Ceres; for the Romans, Demeter, while their daughter Persephone or Proserpina, forced to spend half the year below ground with Pluto, but now personifying the actual crop, was called 'the harvest maiden'. 'Harvest goddess' was a title given too to Diana Artemis for the role she was thought to play in stimulating the luxuriant growth of crops. Festivals and ceremonies were held not only at harvest time but throughout the year at crucial periods in the agricultural calendar, to help ensure that the deities were placated, and so encourage a healthy yield. When to everyone's relief the harvest was finally brought in, it was a time for great celebration. Harvest festivals have been held for thousands of years. In Rome, the *pyanepsia* involved sheaves of wheat with fruits and berries, olive branches and sprigs of bay, along with pastries, honey and wine, being carried in procession to the temple of Apollo. And in Greece, the festivals of *thalusia* too featured the parading and formal presentation of large baskets of fruit and flowers in honour of Demeter.

What was the human thinking behind the origins of some of the ancient gods and goddesses of the crops? Like all the characters of mythology they were inspired by the subconscious awareness of man's descent from the world of hunter-gatherer into the more superstitious world of the farmer. Some are simply representative of the weather, or of the sunshine needed for a good harvest, such as Apollo. Others were more complex. Take Dagon for instance, already mentioned as revered by the Philistines who settled in the land of Canaan. Reminiscent of the gods of the sea, Dagon was visualised as a giant man-like figure with a fish's tail, reminding us that the people largely depended on their fishing as well as their corn harvest. how did Dagon come about? In common with all the Semitic tribes at that time, they recognised the local Baal – the spirit or genius of their lands – on whose whim everything ultimately depended: he was simply 'the lord', the abstract presence to whom they might pray – indeed, we might say now, the highest part of their own inner selves. Baal of course was a wholly male principle, and in order to persuade him to ensure adequate food supplies for the community, the people reasoned that the intervention of a feminine influence was desirable. Accordingly they called on the goddess Astarte (symbolised for them by the planet Venus) to intercede on their behalf. Resulting from the imagined meeting between male and female elements, as the third factor of the triad, the outcome was 'the blessed son of nourishment' as they called Dagon, representing the principle of abundance and a full larder, a bi-specialist god-figure able to oversee equally the fortunes of the cornfield and the fishing grounds.

Almost everywhere in the ancient world, the ultimate god of the harvest – the father of them all – was none other than Kronos, or Saturn, the well-known Father Time. Kronos and his envisioned personality blend imperceptibly into the character of Chronus, the material principle of death and decay: Kronos or Cronus, Chronus, Saturn and Saturnus may have started out as distinct and separate, but they soon became indistinguishable, all represented as the familiar old man carrying a scythe or a sickle. He represents a tying together of the cyclic principles of seed-sowing, cultivation and harvest, and the inevitability of time rolling on through birth, death and decay.

The well-known festivals of the *saturnalia* were held in late autumn or early winter, long after the harvest was safely gathered in, and in some lands these were the main holidays of the year. Everyone was considered equal in the *saturnalia*: nobles sat down with peasants, masters waited upon their servants at table. As well as the banquets, religious sacrifices were made; sporting events and gambling games (using nuts as pieces) were held in the god's honour; theatrical shows were staged; everybody drank freely, and it was a popular occasion for children too, as they were given presents and a holiday from school.

The Living Harvest

If Kronos or Saturn, as the principle of time and its inevitable outcome, was the great father of the growing season and its result – the harvest – Demeter was surely the great mother of these things. Not only was she one aspect at least of 'mother earth', she was also the mother of Plutus, the god of worldly wealth (not Pluto, god of the underworld) and of Persephone or Proserpina, who in the fable is annually carried off by Pluto to Hades. Her alternative Roman name was Ceres, and as the mother goddess of agriculture, she was also known as Deo, 'the grain mother' or 'great corn spirit', and as Chloe, 'the green one'. She is closely connected with the other major goddesses of earth and nature, such as Gaia and Cybele. Sprouting corn festivals dedicated to Demeter were held in early spring, but more important was the annual fasting ceremony at harvest time: then the women of a farming area would fast for nine days to represent the seed lying helpless in the ground; after this time, wearing traditional long white dresses wreathed with stalks and ears of barley and wheat, they would offer up the first fruits of harvest in a festival of thanksgiving. A sow would be sacrificed in the goddess's honour, and this was eaten, washed down with ale made from the newly fermented grain. When pleased, Demeter brought prosperity and fertility to the land, and equally, when angry, she could cause famine – because she was of course a personification of the powers of nature itself.

In Egypt it was Isis, as the principal goddess of the land, who represented the receptive and generative principle in nature, procreation and birth, and through the necessity of irrigation, the fertility of the land and of plants, and ultimately the quality of the harvest. As the sister-wife of Osiris and the mother of Horus, she was undisputed queen of both heaven and earth, of the sea and the underworld. She was usually depicted in ancient art as a veiled queen wearing cow's horns, and besides the cow her sacred symbols were all horned beasts, the crescent moon, the sacred Egyptian ankh device, flowers of all kinds, especially the blue waterlily or lotus of the Nile, the cornucopia, and ears of corn. She was thought responsible for the annual Nile flood and its beneficial effects on the land, and thus the entire harvest. The Egyptian peasant farmers held various ceremonies in her honour, and she was also recognised as a popular nature and harvest goddess in Europe, particularly Rome. In all centuries since, the world over, to 'lift the veil of Isis' has meant to penetrate a great spiritual mystery.

The Celts had Rosmerta as their guardian of grain crops and general food supplies. She became firmly established probably in Neolithic times, when agriculture was taking the place of hunting and gathering as a way of life, when the mysterious stone circles of ancient Britain were being laid out to mark not only the cycle of nature but also family or tribal ownership of land for the first time.

The Scandinavians called upon the earth goddess Frigg, the 'mother of the world', and the two goddesses of their harvest home

THE CYCLE OF NATURE

and seasonal produce, Frey and Nertha. In their warlike way the Vikings staged mock battles between the seasons – their celebration of the cycle of nature – and toasted the inevitable outcome with their customary feasting and revelry.

The Romans were more complicated people than the forthright northerners, and tended to have a deity in waiting for every possibility, and included as many as they could think of when calling down blessings on their harvest. There was Ops, goddess of fertility and abundance, and all good things which came from the earth. As one of the wives of Saturn, she represented fruition in the fullness of time, and thus was associated with the harvest. During the *saturnalia* her own festival was called the *opalia*, when everyone remembered the dormant seed awaiting germination, prostrating themselves and pressing their hands upon the ground. When the harvest itself was nearing completion, they would call upon Annona, 'the provident', to ensure the safe storage of the grain. With her symbols of a wheatsheaf or ears of wheat, and a cornucopia, she was goddess of foodstuffs in general, particularly agricultural produce.

The Greek farming community made much of their god-demon, Agatho-daemon, who, as spirit of the cornfields, equally at home in the heavens as in the underworld, was capable of bringing good harvests or, if he felt neglected or insulted, disastrous blights. In art he was represented as a youth holding a cornucopia and a bowl, sitting amidst poppies and ears of corn.

If the harvest failed completely, anywhere in the world where irrigation was not possible, it was usually because the rains had failed to materialise. A fable tells of Erysichton, 'the tearer up of earth', a mythical character who was cursed for cutting down trees in a grove sacred to Demeter. As a result he was made to suffer the perpetual pangs of hunger, symbolising famine following the disastrous failure of crops. When the ancient promise of abundant harvests given to mankind by Demeter and Persephone failed to materialise, it was probably through no fault of theirs. It was useful to have a supernatural miscreant to blame for the disaster.

Amongst all the gods and goddesses of vegetation and animal life at the service of farmers in the ancient world, those who worked to establish fertility in their crops and livestock would call first upon Priapus, their favourite god of procreation, favoured even above the great Pan or Faunus. With parents like Aphrodite and Dionysus, you would expect Priapus to be active in the field of procreation, and he was of course the personified symbol of male sexuality. He represented the principle of reproductive power and fertility, and this applied with equal importance to all who dealt with the land and relied upon its potentially fruitful nature. He was considered a nature god with special interests in horticulture and vineyards, animal breeding and beekeeping, and inevitably of the corn harvest too. Wooden statues of Priapus were set up in fields and gardens over southern Europe, depicting the rampant god-figure holding a club and a sickle. Sometimes these 'totem poles' were simplified to mere phallic symbols. On a personal level too his significance was not lost, and in later years his name became synonymous with lasciviousness, pornography and lewd behaviour. Jack donkeys were thought to symbolise his nature, and were sometimes sacrificed in his name.

Dionysus, or Bacchus Dionysus, is also of course a god of luxuriant fertility, but his name is more usually associated with the vine and wine-drinking, and he was visualised as wandering through the vineyards, woods and fields, surrounded by a retinue of nymphs and tipsy satyrs. But his power was serious and very real to his followers, and he was said to be severe on those who abused or opposed him, and kind and gentle and the bringer of happiness and quiet blessings on those who accepted him whole-heartedly (which I suppose is more or less the nature of wine itself). Celebrations known as the *dionysia* or *bacchanalia* were held in his honour at various times of the year, throughout the Mediterranean region and whole Roman Empire. In the autumn the sampling of the new wine was a favourite occasion for his faithful followers, and early in the spring the peasant farmers would hold further *dionysia* to celebrate the annual deliverance of the land from the grip of winter, and the swelling of buds on the vine. His symbols included the vine with its leaves and bunches of grapes, and also the similarly shaped evergreen leaves of the ivy.

Largely through its association with Bacchus Dionysus and its vine-like but evergreen nature, ivy came to symbolise eternal life. It is also a very beautiful plant with its dark glossy green foliage, delicate white flowers in late summer and autumn, and black berries to follow. As a constituent of the forest, as a ground-coverer, as a climber, ivy may seriously be considered one of the most valuable of woodland plants, giving evergreen shelter to numerous small creatures, and providing a warm overcoat for the deciduous trees. Many people suppose ivy to harm the tree on which it grows, but this is totally false. It is in no way parasitic, and (unlike the pernicious honeysuckle) its stems yield without constricting the tree trunk as it expands. To understand even this is, in some small way, to put the cycle of nature into its proper perspective.

The evergreen cycle of life was a theme which permeated the worship of the druids. They venerated the oak, of course – a deciduous tree. As a 'plant religion', their ceremonies were based on a search for the secret of life continuing throughout winter, during the apparent finality of death, and they were intrigued by the mistletoe, encouraging it to grow high on the majestic oaks within their sacred groves. The mistletoe is a plant firmly associated in people's minds with mystical pagan beliefs and customs, and in various non-druidic lands too mistletoe has frequently featured in mythological accounts of gods, goddesses and heroes. During winter it certainly is fascinating, mysteriously rooted in the branches when the host trees are leafless and apparently lifeless, miraculously retaining its green leaves and its white moon-like berries on those golden-hued twigs. Such a plant may well seem to carry the greenness of the tree and hold it secure over the barren season, until the arrival of spring rebirth. It may well seem to represent the soul of the tree for those whose lives were still lived close to nature, and it came to symbolise their own souls too.

More directly, the mistletoe symbolised and still symbolises continuity. Even through hard times when the ground is barren and the larder bare, it promises a resurgence of nature's bounty. For many centuries, sprigs of mistletoe have been hung up over doorways and in various other places inside buildings to help this process along: for the farmer, to ensure lush crops and healthy lambs and calves, or simply to promote good luck. For the householder and urban dweller, a reminder of the obligation to reproduce, to be fruitful and multiply – a stolen kiss under the mistletoe is an innocent expression of hoped-for romance. Originally the custom demanded that the man plucked a berry when he won a kiss, and when there were no berries left, the kissing had to stop.

To the Celtic druids mistletoe was obviously associated chiefly with their favourite namesake tree and life-symbol, the oak, and strict rules surrounded its treatment. Sprigs could only be cut by the official druid in charge of the grove, wielding a golden sickle – the *cryman aur* – and when cut, the sprigs were not allowed to fall to the ground. They dropped or were handed down into a white sheet held above the ground – the spotless white sheet symbolising purity and transformation to immortality; the ground signifying death.

Mistletoe can of course be seen growing parasitically on many other kinds of trees besides oak, which is not its commonest host in the British Isles. It is more often to be seen on willows and poplars, lime and hawthorn, and it loves apple trees. There are various species of mistletoe in various lands, but the fabled one is *Viscum album*. If you want to grow your own plant-symbol of eternal life, crush and smear ripe berries directly on the tree bark, leaving the heart-shaped seeds to germinate, and it will take three or four years to establish itself vigorously.

Death and Rebirth

Symbols of cyclic life have been drawn from various points around the full circle: from seed, germination, growth, flowering and fruiting, to seed again. Fruit have always seemed a particularly potent symbol, from mistletoe berries, to pomegranates, to apples. The gods – the passions and expectations of nature personified – were said to keep a supply of golden apples which they ate to restore their own youth, and myths tell how the natural life of the world suffered when they were deprived of these: plants would die, only to spring up again, renewed, when the supply was resumed. Legends abound in southern Europe, telling of this ancient symbol of eternal youth with characters such as the fleet-footed Atalanta, Aphrodite, Cybele, and the Hesperides. In Scandinavia too there are legends of golden apples, jealously guarded for the gods by Iduna, the watchful goddess of spring regrowth.

But mere humans have no miraculous golden apples to keep them young, or to ensure that their lives continue even after the body dies. If 'winter' symbolises death, so 'evergreen' symbolises life enduring – the holly and ivy famously so. Our familiar Christmas tree shows that the evergreen symbol is thriving even today. Since ancient times coniferous trees such as the pine, or its equivalent in different lands, have been considered powerful symbols of immortality.

Evergreen trees are often quite strongly scented – some kinds have provided material to be burnt as incense. Inevitably perhaps, certain evergreens have become associated with death and funeral rites. Cypress trees in particular were associated in the ancient world with funerals and graveyards, and thence with the underworld and its dead inhabitants. Whilst the pine had been held sacred to all the gods of nature, the cypress was considered a sacred symbol of Pluto as god of the underworld, and consequently strongly connected with death and burial. The goddess of graveyards was the enchantress-goddess Hecate who, through the medium of moonlight, watched over the graves. She was reputed to be able to call up the hounds of the underworld to pursue anyone who desecrated these places, for there were mindless vandals about even in those days. Cypress trees were planted as a symbol of mourning, rather than an expression of hope that souls would live on through the winter of death. In more northerly lands yew trees take the place of cypresses, and of course the yew is still strongly associated with all these things. On more practical terms, the yew was extensively planted to supply strong, pliable timber for the manufacture of longbows, and as it is somewhat poisonous to livestock, a churchyard is one of the safest places in which to plant it. It is one of the few trees capable of growing for two thousand years or more.

Death, the underworld, vegetation, spring growth and rebirth, are all inextricably combined. As the 'invisible', or the 'unseen', Hades can be understood in either of two senses: as the abode of shades of the dead, a gloomy place from which there was no escape; or as a name for the god of the dead – a personification indeed of the state of death itself. As a god, Hades was said to be a son of Kronos, with his dual function of time and the harvest, and the consort of Persephone or Proserpina, the vegetation goddess. As a mythical person, identified with Pluto; as a general term for the nether regions, Hades has been identified with Tartarus, though this is often considered to be a lower world still – a world from which even the spirit of vegetation is barred. Through and around these unseen lands were said to flow the Styx, 'the river of hate', Cocytus, 'the river of cries', Periphlegethon, 'the river of fire', and Lethe, 'the river of forgetting'.

It was Pluto or Hades, stern and pitiless, impervious to petition or sacrifice, who owned the three-headed guard dog, Cerberus. The entrance to the underworld of Hades, fabled to lie on the west bank of the earth-encircling river Oceanus, at the very edge of the world, was said to be concealed in a grove of willows, poplars and cypresses, the ground covered with narcissus and asphodel – a plant associated in the ancient world with graveyards. Deep in the darkness below the earth, the underworld of Hades was thought to control everything of value that rises from the ground. It was an inseparable part of the annual cycle of plant life as it dies down in autumn to re-grow and reappear in the spring. Demeter or Ceres, by whichever name the principle is the same, as the mother of Proserpina or Persephone, was goddess of the dead as well as presiding over everything that appears to die in the autumn, only to be brought back to life again in the spring – not only annual vegetation, but also hibernating animals (and particularly the dormouse, which to the Romans was a much-prized delicacy).

It was during the great human descent from the animal-soul to the plant-soul that people first began to ponder on the drama of birth, life and death, when their thoughts dwelled upon the mystery of life somehow continuing after death. Thinkers began to search for reassurance, and before long the dreamers and philosophers among them visualised a 'dying god' who could represent their own spirit, share their experience of death, and sink to the same unknown realms of the underworld, eventually coming to life again as the resurrected, quickened soul. For them the earthly cycle of nature, and most intimately the harvest upon which all ultimately depended, with the seasonal death of vegetation, the dormant period, the sowing of seed followed by spring regrowth, was seen to represent the human dimension of death, burial, and the hope of spiritual resurrection. Such hopes and fears surrounding the cyclic life of our planet became crystallised in religious teachings from all over the globe, ranging from the Christian message of the Lord who died on our behalf, to the Hindu conviction wherein:

The flow and interflow of earthly souls is like a multicoloured tapestry which God weaves, spreading it over the living world, and withdrawing it at will.

The Embodiment of Nature

Generations of people whose lives have been lived close to the soil have prayed to invoke the spirits of the seasons (however these may have been disguised), and in particular perhaps, depending on their cultural expectations for spirits, ancestors or saints, have called upon their own personal god or goddess who might be relied upon to intervene in the machinations of fate. To invoke the spirits of the rebirth of vegetation and the fertility of the soil, was equally to invoke the spirit of death, and the hope of intercession with the keepers of the underworld. The invocation itself may have been personal and quiet, or loud and official, strengthened through the vehemence of ritual and sacrifice, but the hope and the wish were the same and equally dual natured: that the cycle might continue; that the dead and dying might be reborn as heavenly children, from the womb of mother earth.

Demeter or Ceres was the classical 'earth goddess' who possessed the divine capability of interceding with the heavenly hierarchy. But such intercession had to wait till spring; in winter she was no more than goddess of the dead. As co-ruler of the underworld she was also known as 'the black one' or 'the avenger', the arbiter who ensured that the dead received their just deserts. In ancient art Demeter has sometimes been depicted wearing a horse's head: in Greek legend she was pursued into the underworld by Poseidon, god of the watery deep, and changed herself into a mare and galloped away through labyrinths of the underworld. But he, having like Neptune an affinity with horses, changed himself into a stallion and galloped after her, caught up, and mated with her. As a result she gave birth to a miraculous horse – the spirit of fertility.

Her daughter Persephone or Proserpina personified the seed, sown in the earth to disappear from sight and apparently die, to germinate and flourish again in the spring. Together, mother and daughter were known as 'the great goddesses', and various festivals involving flowers and the annual regrowth of vegetation were held in their honour. They were sometimes linked with the often orgiastic festivities held in honour of Dionysus, who was sometimes described as 'the child', or outcome of the re-emergence of Persephone from the barren prison of winter. During the feasting and merrymaking the participators would crown themselves with sprigs of myrtle, herbs, water mint and pennyroyal.

THE CYCLE OF NATURE

Now the general term for a handsome young man, Adonis was originally a Middle Eastern god of nature, supposed to have been born from the aromatic bark of a myrtle or myrrh tree. He was loved by Aphrodite, who nurtured and suckled him as a baby. She gave him to Persephone to babysit for her, but Persephone loved him so much that she refused to give him back, and took him with her into the underworld. In another version of the story he was killed by a wild boar, and from his blood sprang the blood-red anemone; but Persephone brought him back to life, with the condition that he spend half the year with her. As a vegetation spirit, Adonis was recognised in many countries, and the annual feast of Adonis featured 'Adonis gardens' in containers cultivated by the women, and which they dedicated to the god by throwing them into a lake or the sea.

They were typically annual flowers and herbs which were sown and tended in honour of Adonis, the 'god beloved of women', and many medicinal herb gardens were named after him, and not merely by pagans. The people of Damascus by 700 BC were supposed to have abandoned that sort of thing in favour of their own national God of the Israelites, but they retained the practise along with other pagan customs and were berated by the prophet Isaiah who (from a farming background himself) cried out in his exasperation: "Plant then, if you will, your gardens in honour of Adonis; strike your cuttings for a foreign god!"

A Middle Eastern 'dying god' of annual vegetation and its regrowth in spring, and who has sometimes been identified with Adonis, was Tammuz. In his mythical life story he was another personification of death through the vegetation which dies down for winter, and resurrection through its regrowth in the spring. In his case he was the brother of Ishtar or Venus, who was obliged to descend into the underworld each winter to bring him back to life. His many titles include 'the faithful son', 'the resurrected child', 'the son of promise', 'the shepherd', 'lord of the flood', 'plant father', and 'god of the date palm'. He was considered to be the husband of Innini, the 'queen of the fields'.

Triptolemus was a god-hero of the ancient Greeks, and one of the many mythical personalities credited with the original introduction of the practice of sowing and cultivating grain. He was said to have been sent by Demeter to travel the world and spread his knowledge to all lands. The grain-producing areas of his homeland used to be known as 'the threshing-floor of Triptolemus'. In common with many other gods and goddesses of vegetation and agriculture, through his influential place in the underworld, he has sometimes been considered a judge of the dead.

Another 'dying god' who is born again each year, representing the transition from autumn to winter and from winter to spring, was Attis, the pine tree spirit venerated in ancient Turkey and as far afield as Rome. He could well be identified with Adonis, and he too is connected with the rites of Dionysus. As a handsome human youth jealously pursued by the goddess Cybele, he is said to have sacrificed his own manhood at the base of a pine tree, and from the blood that trickled into the ground violets sprang up to clothe the base of the tree. His spirit is supposed to have been taken up by the pine tree, whose evergreen foliage symbolises his survival over the bleakness of winter. For several centuries spring festivals were held in his honour, featuring carnival processions of evergreen branches and pine logs wreathed with violets.

Then there is the story of Hyacinthus, the youth loved by the sun god Apollo, who taught him how to throw the discus. Out of jealousy Zephyrus, the west wind, drove the flying discus against the boy's head, killing him. In the place where he died the original hyacinth flower sprang up from his blood. His character again personifies the idea of vegetation that dies in the autumn and grows again in the spring.

To the ancient Egyptians the representative of the annual death and rebirth of vegetation was Osiris, the epitome of regenerative power, symbolised by the mythical black bull Apis. In the summer his traditional colour was green, symbolising resurrection; in winter it was black, symbolising death. With his son Horus, 'the reborn child' connected with the sky and the sun, he expressed and I suppose still expresses the hope of rebirth for the human soul in a higher form.

In Asia Minor, Sabazius was the god of nature and its fullness, sinking as a 'dying god' in winter, and rising again in the spring. The many gods of ancient Mesopotamia too included several associated with the restoration to life of vegetation dying each autumn to be reborn in the spring, nature deities whose attributes were called upon to restore human souls after death. Such as Ninurta, Ninkarrak, Gatumdug, and Nindindug: all different, with their own mythical life stories, all the same in their significance – human hopes and fears with regard to the cycle of nature, and how this cycle should relate to human destiny.

As in the Christian parable: 'seed does not come to life unless it has first died ... sown in the earth as a perishable thing it is raised imperishable'. It is only natural to look for ways to turn so impersonal a principle into a personal, practical possibility. But not all are 'born again' Christians, or devout Moslems with their conviction of a paradise to come. Many people nowadays seize upon the idea of reincarnation as something to be desired. But reincarnation is not a conscious process, and it cannot be made conscious because the mind is not privy to it. The dawning of spiritual consciousness blows away reincarnation like a forgotten dream. There can be no reincarnation for the conscious soul, and as the whole process is necessarily unconscious there can be little comfort in it. By such means one can attain neither the light of heaven, nor even the light of the subtle wisdom zone of materiality.

Cycling endlessly from life to life within nature is fine for animals and plants, but there comes a time, as the development of the inner self progresses through the long night and we are fortunate enough to approach the possibility of finding that unseen path of which the patriarch Job spoke, and described in the Upanishads as the path to eternity trodden by sages, we come to realise that reincarnation is not what human beings are destined for.

The mind that flits like a butterfly through the garden of desires, sipping here and there and caring not for the future, flies to life and death again in a never-ending cycle.

A caterpillar, coming to the end of its leaf, reaches across and gains another leaf. The soul, leaving one body behind, reaches across and gains another body.

There are three great powers in nature, created to govern the minerals, the plants, and the animals. When the soul of man is governed also by these powers, he strays blindly along the paths of illusion, wandering endlessly from death to death.

There is no heaven for people within the cycle of nature. The path to heaven follows the direction of evolution, from the material world of rocks and minerals, through the plant kingdom, through the animal kingdom and the human zone, to the dawn awakening of the spiritual worlds beyond. There are no 'passions' there. A heaven of the passions would have to be an animal heaven, a plant heaven, a material heaven: these are what are known as paradises, still within the laws of nature and materiality. People who live mainly within one of the soul-levels of nature, wherever their soul is strongest, most firmly attached, may well enter the paradise of that zone when their life on earth comes to an end. People who are still descending, still part-way along their journey of the passions, are limited to those levels which they have traversed. If you read the Old Testament, for instance, you will find little mention and no expectation or personal concept of 'heaven'. Though the people then were still comparatively high in their spiritual status, lacking the balance provided by the lower levels of nature, when they died, they either 'rested with their ancestors', or they went to 'sheol', which sounds unpleasant, but can really mean whatever you want it to mean. The soul has to complete its downwards journey and acquire an even mix of 'passions' before it can rise, and there is far more choice for people nowadays. For those who have reached the soul-level of materiality, their destiny will depend upon faith, and on the direction towards which that faith is orientated.

THE CYCLE OF NATURE

Only when we have completed what for us must represent the full cycle of nature, having explored and experienced the whole gamut of 'passions', descending to each stage of soul-level in turn – the, human, the animal, the plant, the material – and then, the cycle only half complete, to ascend from the material, through the plant, through the animal and the human levels again, finally to reach the non-material levels of spiritual being. Only then will we be in a position to speak of 'heaven'. Passions carry us down from the innocence of childhood; the very antithesis of passion – submission to those unseen spiritual powers from whence we came – can carry us back up. And only then, having lived through the whole world of nature, can we acquire the inner balance typified by 'compassion', the coming-together of everything to be known about our own human condition.

Faith may be a 'passion' but it is the very best passion within the material level, and it can certainly indicate one's potential destiny. 'Faith can move mountains', so we are told, and in this case the mountain will be the very solid bulk of universal materiality. Faith directed towards material things will guide the soul into ever denser realms of materiality. Faith directed towards the divine should at the very least hold the soul in readiness to make the ultimate return journey to the starting point of the newborn child, and thence beyond into saintly and angelic realms. This journey will constitute the condition known to Catholics as 'purgatory' – the process of shedding the weight of passions from the soul which in effect can become progressively lighter, allowing it to rise along with the flow of creation, to climb back up the subtle ladder of nature in the abstract – the ladder to heaven of Jacob's dream.

Can you turn faith on like a tap? Indeed, I don't know. But in cases where there is no faith with which to orientate the soul, it may not be unlucky enough to become merged with the heavy layers of materiality, but neither will it be fortunate enough to set out on the great ascent. As described so tellingly in the Revelation of John the Divine, it will be 'neither hot nor cold'; unconscious and unaware, it will go neither up nor down, and its fate may well be that which we call reincarnation. As most of us live largely within the spiritual zone of materiality, and enjoy its benefits, its advantages, it would seem to make sense for us to locate that little pocket of faith which we all should have, and direct it away from further material gains, towards the lost innocence of Eden – towards the long-lost realm of spirit.

CHAPTER NINE

Forest and Mountain

WILD NATURE DOES NOT SLEEP. It is at night that the apparently inanimate forms of rocks and trees seem to come to life, especially at the touch of moonlight. The ancient goddess of wild nature, whether we call her Diana, or Hecate, or Selene, or by one of a myriad other names, through her magical silver light quickened rocky peaks and deep forests, penetrated rarely trod mountain passes, mesmerised the birds and beasts and enchanted the human inhabitants.

Some see it like that even today. In the form of moonlight ranging over the earth, the goddess looks favourably on the ancient stone circles and sacred groves, the hallowed ground of previous ages, on forest rides and haunted marshes, and by touching them enhances their mysterious beauty. It was the same goddess who visited the innumerable sacred altars described in the scriptures, half darkness and half light beneath the spreading terebinth trees of ancient Palestine. Her followers then – as some do now – invoked her presence to waken the spirits of trees and rocks and springs, to embrace the cool birches and ash trees dappled silver in her light, touching sensuously the dark and fragrant bark of the pines, taking pleasure in the rugged masculinity of an ancient oak. Fauns and dryads under her influence rubbed sleep from their eyes, shook the dew from their tresses, and went about their nightly affairs.

> *When black-cupp'd crocus show their silver tips*
> *The sleeping satyr stirs and thrills to Hecate's caress.*

In ancient Greek myth there was once a handsome shepherd boy called Endymion, who used to lead his flocks into the high mountain pastures to graze. The goddess Selene used to watch him in the evenings as she peeped over the mountain top, and fell hopelessly in love with him – a mortal loved by an immortal, separated by the gulf of invisibility. In despair she approached Zeus and entreated him to make Endymion immortal too so that her love could be consummated. Zeus granted her request, but with a cruel twist. It was still doomed to be a one-sided affair, for the god stipulated that, as the price of immortality, Endymion should remain asleep for ever. Since then, in her guise as the moon, Selene has visited him nightly where he sleeps alone in his mountain grotto, and there embraces him tenderly in the form of moonlight.

The spirit of wilderness can exert a powerful pull over humans who fall under its spell, and it is not merely the romance of moonlit rocks and trees that calls them. Is it an urge to commune and be one with nature, or simply a form of disillusionment, a burning desire to be alone? Our own privileged overall view of the spiritual forces in nature can give us a clue about that: the lone explorer's intense observation of nature amidst all her wild grandeur, the experience of certain aspects of unsophisticated living, can perhaps put him or her in touch with the human source. Perhaps such experience offers a chance to surmount all those multitudinous instincts that have already interfered too much in all our lives – a place where they really have no right to intrude, but where they were willingly invited by our ancestors in their longing for the comforts of civilisation.

Romantic wilderness

In North America people with this wanderlust in times gone by have referred to the spirit of the wendigo: an unseen but strongly-felt spirit of the wilderness whose presence draws men from their sheltered bunks and sets them on a lone trail through the northern forests, among snow-capped mountains and ice-fringed lakes. The wendigo, it is said, can travel over the tops of the forest trees so fast that the leaves or conifer needles are singed and seared, giving off puffs and plumes of smoke. You can well imagine this weird spirit of the wild in the spring, when the forest birds are beginning to make their nests, when the snow and ice are fast melting, and the sun warming daily entices the wanderer out from his winter retreat. When you climb a hill and look over the tops of a pine forest, you will see little gusts of wind stirring the pine branches. Whipped up by local extremes of temperature, with pockets of hot and cold air here and there, the playful breeze causes little puffs and thicker clouds of pine pollen which leaves airy trails like smoke, cutting across the hillsides and swirling through the valleys.

The New World of the Americas has its own remembered histories and fables told by its indigenous peoples. In Europe and Asia too, in ancient times, the forest typified untamed land and wild nature, where people hunted for food and gathered the necessities for life. The forest indeed was not an alien or frightening place as it may have seemed to some people since, but a workplace, a communally-shared field of operations.

Numerous gods and goddesses of nature it seems were appointed to preside over human involvement in the world of wild creatures, and over hunting in particular. The wisest among the people knew full well that they needed to be able to exploit nature to the full, without upsetting its fine balance. In general terms hunters, and everyone else who lived and worked in the forest, assumed that they were protected from day to day by friendly supernatural beings, such as satyrs – half man, half goat, spirits of woodland and mountain, followers of the nature god Bacchus or Dionysus. Like their human dependants they could be crafty, drunken, and lustful; they played music on their reed pipes and chased voluptuous nymphs through the trees: the satyrs truly represented the human-animal soul of the hunters and woodsmen in the forest, and in later years the farmers and herdsmen; they were 'just like us' because, in truth, they *were* us. They represented the subtle side of *our own* passions.

For serious matters, when truly divine intervention was needed, prayers were directed to a *real* god or goddess, and the favourite deity of hunters and country people everywhere was

Diana Artemis. One of her many titles was *Agrotera*, 'the wild wanderer', referring to her role as nature goddess with special responsibility for the lives of wild animals, in whose company she was said to roam the hills and forests. She was principally a European goddess; the equivalent goddess of nature further east was called Ma. She too ran through the forests with the wild beasts, and looked after their welfare as well as that of the hunters. By day she was said to walk over the Taurus Mountains, but watched over human and animal affairs at night, from her throne in the moon. Diana Artemis, of course, was closely identified with the moon, and the other moon goddesses such as Selene and Hecate were also thought to be involved in the business of hunting and conserving natural resources. Inevitably so, for the moon itself watched over the forest very vividly, its light piercing nightly the forest fastness, or seeming to chase the clouds scudding across the sky.

Hunting is no longer a necessity for human life, and hunting for pleasure has only recently become a controversial subject: the present-day equivalent of 'hunting' (when sheer sentiment is set aside) might be concern for the environment – the wish to become involved and to profit from nature while sustaining it, or leaving it richer than before in natural resources, rather than to impoverish it, whether through ignorance or neglect or wilful uncaring. All hunting deities in ancient times were also concerned with the wild animals' welfare, their health and freedom to breed prolifically. This is really an important point to bear in mind. Even today, traditional 'hunting, shooting and fishing' can have a beneficial effect, if they are part and parcel of the balance of nature and the vigorous life of the earth.

When things went wrong, as of course they often did, there was no shortage of supernatural troublemakers living in the forest who could be made to take the blame. Who was Fatuus, 'the joker', 'the mischievous one' who sent strange dreams to anyone who fell asleep in his woods? None other than the great Pan, also known as Faunus. He was able by his sudden appearance to cause panic in man or beast. He had horns and goat's feet, but he was above the satyrs in supernatural status, a god of prophecy who could send meaningful dreams of the future, and was worshipped accordingly in groves and grottos and beneath spreading trees. Unlike the imp-like fauns of the forest he was not displaced or defeated when the spread of farming meant the destruction of his forest lands – he simply moved into the newly developed farmlands and took over as resident god of farm animals, flocks and herds, as well as the woods and hills. In ancient art he has usually been depicted carrying the reed pipes or syrinx, and sometimes a shepherd's crook, frequently a garland of pine leaves and cones, and a bunch of grapes. In early farming days regular sacrifices of milk and honey, rams and lambs and nuts were made to him. All in all, Pan was the personification of the passion that fills men who are familiar with the forest, and who leave the woodsman's life to cultivate pasturelands and rear animals.

Provided there were plenty of trees left standing, in shelterbelts, hedgerows or groves, Pan could bring his children with him to help in tending the herds, especially the cattle and the pigs. These children, the 'imps of the forest', were the paniskoi or fauns, mischievous, miniature versions of himself. Left to their own devices they could lead astray travellers in the forest; but properly controlled they were to be credited with much useful work herding the animals. These were animal gods, of course. Plant gods – like the dreaded Erl-king or alder king who was first envisaged in Germany and said to lure little children to their deaths – whether deities, demons or goblins, stayed in the forest and would not venture out into the farmlands. The true goblins or roguish sprites have usually been thought to live in hollow trees, within cavities beneath tree roots, but with a great fondness for old ruined stone buildings which are covered in ivy, and they usually avoid contact with humans. But another forest-dwelling imp-demon, the hobgoblin, also known as Puck or Robin Goodfellow, whilst living in the forest, often visits human habitations.

Where the forest runs into hills and mountains, the supernatural populations have tended to change to suit the terrain.

Pan of course changed his nature enough to allow him to look after the shepherds and goatherds who tended their flocks in the hill pastures, and in that environment he was often known as Lupercus – the protector of flocks from attacks by wolves. The shepherds' *lupercalia* festivals during the lambing season invoked Pan's presence, and involved various magical means of keeping predators at bay whilst their lambing ewes were at their most vulnerable.

All this was practical stuff, tinged with superstitious respect for the supernatural; but the undisguisedly romantic perceptions of the people were as strong as ever, with the graceful nymphs of hills and mountains – oreads to the Greeks, and similar divinely attractive beings in other lands. Wild and rocky terrain was thought to be the favourite playground of the goddesses of heaven, such as Hera, the heavenly queen. Her worshippers would climb up their local mountain to offer her praise. In Asia Minor the equivalent goddess was Rhea or Cybele, 'great mother of the gods', and her worshippers would form torchlight processions over hills and through the forests, playing music and dancing until they were exhausted. The moonlight goddess Selene too was powerfully associated with hills and mountains, which were considered sacred to her. But such places in ancient times were also, and perhaps especially, considered strongholds of the wilder deities of nature: such as Bacchus Dionysus, whose followers would gather and hold what were reputed to have been unrestrained orgies in some of the wildest of places. Some of these gatherings are said to have been for women only, with menfolk strictly precluded. Further east in the hills above Mesopotamia, the people celebrated two great deities, Imkhursag, 'wind of the mountains', and Nintud, 'queen of the mountain'. And overall, of course, from the Atlantic to the Urals, Diana Artemis was praised and celebrated in the hilltops as the undisputed 'wild wanderer' of nature.

The Persian god-creator of light and earthly wisdom, Mithras, was identified with the sun god of other lands. Mithras was also considered the god of rocky places and caves into which, it was believed, the souls of the dead went down before finally rising to the light, and so he too was worshipped in the mountains, in ravines, caverns and underground grottos. Gradually it seems the ancient deities lost their power, and in men's minds the forest gave way to a world of rocks, mines and quarries. A new pattern was set: Human souls perhaps were content to stay amongst the rocks and boulders too. For the first time, supernatural beings became candidly 'material', more openly 'satanic'. The long succession of nymphs, satyrs, fauns, woodland gods and goddesses had not been concepts of materiality; they had personified the supernatural worlds of animals and plants in their spiritual relationship with the human psyche.

As the 'Age of Reason' dawned, rather than gods and goddesses and minor woodland deities, people saw only gnomes, knockers and kobolds, supernatural beings connected with the idea of materiality and the wealth that is obtainable from the earth itself. Traditionally, such creatures of the imagination have been supposed to act as wardens of mines and quarries, guarding the treasures hidden there. Trolls in Scandinavian lands were totally 'material', custodians of precious stones, skilled in metal work, and usually evil in intent. They were seen as stunted and misshapen, as though to reflect the soul's descent through these spiritual layers, from the high human level, through that of the animals, through that of the plants, to the level of minerals, of rock itself, albeit gold-bearing rock. Perceptions of the divine were nearing rock-bottom: the time was approaching for people to think of climbing back, to regain some of their long-lost childish innocence, their original sense of wonder, their guardianship of the world of nature.

Searching for a Hidden Way

Long ago, perhaps, when superstition had scarce begun – that is, when people saw nature as integrated into a whole rather than fragmented into a myriad disparate forms, and consequently had not yet begun to visualise gods and goddesses able to take over their own responsibilities as stewards and stewardesses of nature, perhaps then the idea of seeking 'a way back to heaven' seemed not at all far-fetched. In those days solitary dwellers in the wilderness – hermits in fact – were said to be commonplace. Later, when superstitious personifications of nature had begun to take a hold in men's minds, Buddhism formed an early resistance movement to that process. "If gods exist," the Buddha said, "they must come under the same laws as all else". Materiality as we know it, with all its temptations, its obsession with possessions and consumer goods, had not begun. People then were more 'matter of fact' about the wilderness, and the bodhisattvas – those seeking to become Buddhas – adopted the hermit's way of life in an attempt to avoid imbibing the instinctual temptations that were all around them, the less-than-human vibrations of nature, and the influence of other people less dedicated than themselves.

Do people still feel 'the call of the wild'? Does our present-day generation still feel the unexplained and usually unexpressed yearning for solitude, for aloneness? It used to be a favourite theme, the isolation that can bring one face to face with oneself. Is it simply the need to escape daily routine that a person feels, when they would like to *think* they feel the lure of the wilderness? Plainly, what escapees from civilisation actually experience is something 'different' or unfamiliar, involving 'getting away from it all'. But the media are forever inventing new frontiers to explore, new viewing experiences without us having to take the trouble of actually going anywhere. Most people who feel they need a break from routine seem to end up elbow to elbow on some popular beach, or in an even more crowded club or bar. Anyone might suppose that what most restless people feel is 'desire': a desire for new relationships, for physical pleasure, or for material wealth and good fortune; a desire to search for some undefined treasure buried somewhere 'out there', a search for yet more materiality which can only add to the soul-burden, rather than a genuine need to seek isolation and thereby reappraise one's position in life.

On the face of it, the search for solitude is still a matter of following the emotions, of satisfying the heart, to the same extent that the holidaymaker crowding in amongst all the other holidaymakers is following the emotions, satisfying the heart. The truth of it must be that anyone seeking solitude hopes to experience something *different,* something out of the ordinary and not usually available. And within this sense of difference, the solitude-chaser is sensing none other than his or her own self. The treasure that real deeply-motivated searchers long for is, after all, buried somewhere much nearer home. And of course it may easily turn out that this very 'difference' is the biggest distraction of all, a stumbling block, because that elusive sought-after fortune has been there within ourselves all the time.

The factors that no doubt will have triggered such a search can only be a personal matter for each individual, but whenever someone feels discontented with their lot, hampered by their own limitations, I would hazard a guess that in their daily lives they feel unable to 'be themselves', unable, in other words, to follow their own instincts. In the wilds, leaving civilisation and society behind if only for a little while, the individual can cast off the burden of mundane responsibilities, shedding the need to constantly react in an acceptable manner, the need to observe the sometimes restrictive rules of etiquette and morality, the necessity to 'act a part' the whole time.

Above all, such a person is searching – searching for his or her true self; searching for 'the way'. The two go together, because none but the 'true self' can find or pursue the true 'way'. It is not a matter for the personality; not a matter for determination. In whatever terms these things are couched, in the normal course of events both principles are unknown factors. Both are certainly somewhere to be found; but, we may ask ourselves, is the search to be carried out by means of self analysis – by 'soul searching' – or can it be done by searching physically somewhere 'out there'? The difficulty of even identifying the hidden path of the self was touched upon by Job during his sufferings, expressed forcibly during his long and wonderfully poetic discourse on the mysterious ways of God :

OUR SPIRITUAL JOURNEY

There is a path which no fowl knoweth,
And which the vulture's eye has not seen.
The lion's whelps have not trodden it,
Nor the fierce lion passed by it.

On the face of it, there are two types of 'loners' likely to make for the wilderness, two kinds of hermit (and you might include back-packers and super-tramps in the mould of W. H. Davies in this category): the secular, and the religious, although it is largely a matter of culture and custom. The former, the seemingly more down-to-earth types, have been found mainly among westerners; the latter types, the openly religious seekers, have been been found mainly among easterners. Westerners may of course possess deeply religious motives for seeking solitude, but they tend to use a secular mask to cover their spiritual search: they claim to be studying nature, archaeology, geology, botany, birds, the environment...

Historically, in the Far East, for many centuries there has been a popular tradition (probably almost extinct nowadays) for men, after their family needs have been satisfied, their children grown up and left home, to go off and live in isolation. Such people would openly acknowledge or claim that they were seeking the spiritual side of their lives. They feel the need to find a little piece of wilderness, a niche into which they could fit, to escape worldly influences. Westerners on the other hand, displaying a more practical pioneer spirit, have aimed to take over a piece of wilderness for themselves and tame it. Both east and west have tended to look outwards for the secret of life, whatever their claims of spiritual orientation. But according to ancient Buddhist tradition, only one seeking the highest could hope to combine both elements successfully: to seek within one's own self whilst isolated in the wilds. Who today could even find the opportunity to attempt to live like the bodhisattva in this 7th century poem by the Buddhist monk Shantideva?

FOREST AND MOUNTAIN

Alone and unknown
shall I dwell, in peace and with untroubled mind
Like the new moon will I live my hidden life.

Fain would I dwell
in forest land, beneath a tree, or in a cave,
In disregard for all, ne'er looking back.

Fain would I dwell
'midst leafy rocks owned by no man,
And there, a hermit, follow my own mind.

With a simple bowl;
and a robe that will not tempt a thief;
There will I live exempt from fear and pride.

Alone a man is born;
still more alone he meets his death;
Such anguish none, not even friends, can share.

So will I ever nurture passive solitude,
Welcoming stillness, all distractions stilled.

The vibrations of nature, the instincts being picked up by humankind, the passions that surround everybody and make them 'less than human': these were the influences that the hermit monk was trying to avoid. Worldly influences and temptations were no doubt far fewer many centuries ago than is the case today; but what we have learned tells us that the 'passions' originating from below the truly human level of instinctive life permeate the whole of nature. There was no escape amongst the leafy rocks of the wilderness. Animal, vegetable and mineral, these influences were all around the hermit, in his eyes, his ears, his nose, his mouth, his lungs, his stomach. Along with the rest of the human race, he would have become that much more distracted, more passionate, more influenced. He would probably have been under the sway of an unseen master – the fearsome Asura, god-demon of the forest, eastern equivalent of the western Green Man, shining red as the polarity of green, the infra-red light of the supernatural life of the plant kingdom. The hermit monk had to learn that a desire, a *passion* for patience, accompanied by a feeling of submission to higher powers, are characteristic of the plant life force which is being used by those higher powers: a brand of patience that serves only to cloak the fierce, distrustful, aggressive passions, the natural instincts of the plant kingdom whose way of life he had unconsciously been trying to emulate.

Personally, I am all in favour of visiting places that you consider to be 'wild', and the perception of 'wilderness' is bound to vary from person to person. But I would caution such a visitor not to become too emotional about it. When the opportunity arises, do not miss the chance to drink in and absorb the quiet seasonal beauty of the place, to open yourself to it peacefully, and let it fill your own empty spaces with its beauty. Let yourself experience the truly peaceful: but leave your passions at home.

People of the Groves

In the Celtic world the antlered animal-god Cernunnos ruled almost unchallenged in the wildest forests. Throughout Europe the animal-gods Pan and Faunus also presided over forest lands accompanied by their retinue of imps, but their territory included fields and the countryside in general. The woodpecker god Picus presided over the thinning and felling of forests to make way for the planting of orchards and gardens. Dryads and hamadryads, plant-nymphs of individual trees, came to greater awareness when their forests were worked selectively, cleaned, thinned, felled and replanted. The plant-god of forestry rather than forests was or is Silvanus, presiding over human-controlled and well-ordered forest areas where attention is given to individual trees and their cultivation. Originally Silvanus was the Roman god of woodlands, plantations and groves, guardian of boundaries, hedges and fences set between field and forest. As a god of foresters and woodmen, he watched over the forest edge rather than the wildest thickets. Landowners would dedicate a grove to him.

FOREST AND MOUNTAIN

Whether nature spirits are real to you or not (and to any citizen of the 21st century they will probably not be), whether you accept them or not, their influence nevertheless is real. They are real because they are none other than the emanations of the essence of organic life, the natural instincts, the vital vibrations of the forests and all the life forms which live there. They can be seen, smelled, and heard. Whether you accept the principle of nature's 'vibrations' in this context probably depends on your own interest or lack of interest in the forest ecosystem.

A forest clearing freshly felled will have created a desperate battle ground involving all the plant instincts in and around it. An established forest (especially an indigenous mixed forest) is certainly a peaceful place, but the truce will have been brought about by a natural balance of power. In fact a cold war is in operation, as though prompted by the threat of mutual destruction. When you cut the forest back, or carve out a grove (the words 'grove', 'graven', 'carve' are from the same root) you will have broken the truce and set these powers at each others' throats. You will have invoked the woodland god Silvanus, and handed the reins of control over to him.

Could we but see it, the forest edge, the newly established ride, the clearing, the grove, is positively astir with the vibrations of fierce plant instinct, and some of these vibrations will be taken up and absorbed by that part of your soul that is most sympathetic towards them, most accommodating towards the plant world: the plant-soul in yourself. This will happen quite unconsciously, of course; but your own 'plant passions' will have been strengthened, quickened, and set in motion too. Long ago, this extra surge of passions was probably felt more strongly by those who concerned themselves with such supernatural things and took them seriously. Nowadays at least one good thing to come of it is that people who constantly put themselves into that situation, in the front line of plant warfare – such, shall we say, as forest workers – are strengthened by these instincts and given an extra capacity for hard work, an extra boost of stamina.

Certainly it was customary in the ancient world to dedicate forest groves to the worship of various gods and goddesses, some local, some national, all with the aim of using the extra energy which the people sensed was released there; to strengthen the influence of that deity − to give a boost to whatever seemed important to them at the time. Mysterious gods of nature called the cabiri are said to have been worshipped by the Greeks and their allies, using secret rites in fiercely guarded forest groves. These nature spirits were known to their followers as 'the great ones', and this was their function: to strengthen whatever cause their worshippers brought for their consideration; to give that cause, by way of its human petitioners, an energy-boosting 'injection' of plant instincts.

There were pine groves dedicated to Attis, the god of vegetation which died down in the winter to shoot up again in the spring − a strengthening of the vegetative cycle of nature. There were hazel groves intended to strengthen and draw strength from these valuable little trees, suppliers of nuts, poles, rods, firewood and charcoal, and dedicated to Corylatus, the nut-tree goddess (one of the many titles of the ubiquitous Diana Artemis). All over Europe there were alder groves, the lowland trees which with the willows marked the swampiest valleys and river banks, and greatly valued for numerous uses from ships to shoes. The spirit of *gwernen* − a Celtic name for alder − is said to live on in wild moorland areas long after the trees themselves have gone, instilling energy into passers-by. Poplars and willows were also revered in their own groves for their resilience rather than strength, and these have inspired numerous myths − especially perhaps the weeping willows, symbols of sorrow.

Translation between different languages has sometimes confused sacred groves with standing stones and altars, with the tamarisk and terebinth and other isolated trees, or with the asherah − wooden posts or totem poles set up to mark places of worship in Middle Eastern lands. Northern European goddesses of nature such as the German Holda and the Scandinavian Nerthus or Hertha were worshipped in lonely woodland groves and also, according to available records, around stone cairns set up in rocky places, and various springs and pools. Particularly isolated trees were also thought sacred to these goddesses, regarded with superstitious awe and guarded fiercely.

In general all forest groves within the Roman Empire were considered sacred to Diana Artemis, and oak was clear favourite as the tree for this purpose. (In Rome itself, however, the most famous grove, a carefully tended clump of oak trees on the Capitol hill, was held sacred to the name of Juno, queen of heaven, and inhabited by a flock of geese, fabled guardians of Rome quick to raise the alarm when intruders appeared). In the Roman countryside oak groves were dedicated to Jupiter in addition to Diana, and numerous other local gods and goddesses too. Some of these groves were considered to be oracles, and specialist priests were employed to make predictions by interpreting the rustling of leaves, the notes of birds in the branches, and the rhythmic tinkling of wind-chimes hanging from the twigs.

The Romans brought their respect for the oak to Britain, where they encountered the *real* oak tree people, the Celtic druids – oaks by name, and oaks by nature. The very souls of the Druids, it seems, were as akin to the oak as it was possible for men to be, in their unyielding, unbowed strength of purpose and arrogance of instinct. The druids too established oak groves in which they honoured their deities, and they valued the influences they received very highly. As plant-soul people themselves they revered these strange supernatural vibrations and listened to the fierce whisper of the plants confronted with their own fight for life: suppress or be suppressed; gain the advantage; kill and rule.

The only authority a plant truly accepts in these circumstances is a force greater and stronger and more ruthless than itself, and this of course is exactly what happened when the animal-soul Romans conquered Britain. They saw the oak-loving druids as a threat to their own authority, and stamped them out, beating them down like unwanted vegetation. After some years of persecution, the British Celts abandoned the oak as their spiritual emblem, and adopted the birch tree as their totem plant instead, a more flexible group symbol. A tree of instant expression, one that springs up quickly and just as readily gives way to others, the birch is one of the least 'fierce' trees in the wood. Birch groves became the chapels and meeting places of the Celts, and, seeing no challenge, the Romans had no quarrel with this.

It is no bad thing, perhaps, to find your own balance that allows you to live in the world without upsetting others. The pendulum of karma, we might say, swings slowly and finds its eventual point of balance. It is only natural, and human nature, to find a balance in your way of life: if your work keeps you isolated in wild and lonely places, you will probably feel the need to socialise, to seek the bright lights and cheerful company of civilised surroundings in your spare time. Conversely, if your work and lifestyle keep you in constant contact with others, it will be natural for you to seek a modicum of solitude in your leisure time. Solitude is where you listen rather than talk: listen to wild nature and enjoy it to the full. But above all listen to yourself; your own true nature ought not to be hidden. Even if it turns out to be undesirable or antisocial, it needs to come to the surface, to come into the light and be 'worked through'. The only wilderness to be feared should in truth be the wilderness within. Quietly search that wilderness to find your own true self, for this is the message of all wild nature: Know Thyself!

CHAPTER TEN

Subtle Materiality

ALL THE INSTINCTS, vibrations, or passions of nature may have seemed to be freely independent and unique in every case, but we can see now that they are really subordinate to a much more powerful force, a power which is spiritually 'lower' than themselves, rather than 'higher'. On whatever level they may seem to function, all manifestations of nature are held together and ultimately directed by the force of materiality. Even the most abstract of nature's vibrations, we can say, the subtlest of instincts, are there because the material life forms which they control and from which they emanate, are just that – material forms made up of atoms and so forth. They may be 'supernatural' but they are not really 'spiritual' in the usually accepted sense of the word.

If you consider the universe (or at least that portion of it that we know about) then of course you can see that apparently everything in it, however subtle or however complicated, has this basic nature of materiality: the physical forces of gravity, the production, accumulation and distribution of matter and gases. This is the principle that holds everything together and makes it work, and it follows that no creature of the earth could possibly live in the form we know it without this powerful force; it is utterly necessary for all our lives. And yet this is the force that stands in opposition to spirituality. Spirit is the one force that can function independently of materiality. Spirituality is the condition that is not limited or controlled by atoms or molecules. Spirit permeates the world of atoms as well as the rest of the universe, and it is spirit – or so at least mystics claim – that gives the spark of life to every material life form.

In this broad sense, everything we can see and hear, including the people around us and our own selves, even our own thoughts, are objects or products of materiality. But in the sense that we need to use the term, in the 'common sense', humans are understood to be humans; animals to be animals; plants to be plants. Each life form is equipped with its own life force, but we need to bear this duality of definition in mind. 'Materiality' we must take to mean the force that regulates apparently lifeless material objects, the laws of physics working as though they comprised a set of instincts – the instincts that oblige atoms to gather themselves into specific groups. To take it still further, materiality has to provide the means of developing our power of thought, the ability to use our brains and emotions, and the ability, the understanding to modify and arrange material objects or raw materials in special ways, and form them into all the material goods we have come to rely upon, the things we need and desire. From the material rather than the human instincts comes the need and ability to make and wear clothes and build houses. Animals, being limited to their own animal-type instincts, feel no such need and have no such ability.

These material instincts, these obtrusively heavy, insistent vibrations, have been allowed to play an increasingly powerful role in our minds, sometimes to the extent of taking over our lives completely. As a result we tend to behave in ways calculated to increase our store of materiality: we set our hearts on collecting more and more material products, living in luxury perhaps, becoming wealthy. Constantly wishing for this or that tends to make us greedy – not necessarily 'bad' , though we may sometimes overlook the needs of outsiders in the struggle to satisfy our own needs and those of our own families and dependants. Not 'bad' in itself perhaps, but nevertheless this material force is the power that religious people through the ages have called the 'satanic power' – the apparently evil force that keeps us close to things, keeps our hearts and minds loyal to the things of the earth, rather than to the intangible world of spirit.

It is characteristic of civilisation for humans to possess a spiritual centre of gravity which positions itself within the level of materiality. It is not the same as having a material-soul. In fact, there are whole races of people in the world who, by nature, do have a soul relationship with these material life forces, a spiritual predilection for them, and we could call them material-soul people. Far from having a material centre of gravity and an accompanying accumulation of *things*, these material-soul people tend to be noticeably lacking in the benefits of materiality, and are frequently forced to live in abject poverty and need. Their soul type tends to make them see themselves and each other in some sense as material objects rather than worthy human beings, and this characteristic has encouraged other races in the past to see them as material objects too, to be moved around and bought and sold as though they really were just 'things'.

This is all part of the strange and sometimes contradictory power of Satan, as the personification of the forces of materiality. But it is also a part – the major part – of the world in which we live. The great majority of us are centred one way or another in materiality, so we have to make the best of it. However, if we pay heed to the great religions of the world, we may think that we do not particularly want to be left at Satan's mercy when our lives are over; for us simply to leave it at that does seem to be taking something of a chance. So many of us have come to think that it might not be a bad idea to look for a way out – a way up – along that 'hidden path' which should be somewhere at the root of all ways of searching, at the heart of all religions. And if we can do it without first having to lose our worldly possessions, or lead ascetic lives in the wilderness like the bodhisattva monk, if we can find a way to have 'all this and heaven too' – so much the better.

The Common Descent

This will probably be a good time to recapitulate the nature of spiritual 'levels' and the whole process of spiritual decline: from higher humans to ordinary humans, from humans to animals, from animals to plants, from plants to things. The process following the march of civilisation runs contrary to the actual flow of creation.

The aim of civilisation is to achieve the total benefits of materiality; the aim of Gaia's great dream is a dawn awakening to the spiritual perfection of the human psyche. If 'heaven' is our aim, then in this context 'heaven' must imply a state of pure spirit, free from the influence of materiality. Supposing someone experiences a blissful 'out of body' state and is then able to return and describe it in material terms, if it featured this or that, sights, sounds, feelings, sensations, then we can be pretty sure that it cannot really be 'heaven'. It may well be some sort of 'paradise' concealed somewhere within the world of materiality, and thus still within the sphere of influence of this material force. From what we have already gathered, we can conjecture that an opportunity to experience the states called 'heaven', or 'paradise', or even 'hell', will depend upon the contents or the centre of gravity of the soul.

One's own life in retrospect presents the clearest outline of the civilising process of spiritual descent: when you were newly born, like all babies, you possessed what we think of as the human attributes in potential; they were not yet developed. Your brain at that time was not able to take in all the sights and sounds and impressions of the world around you, and you lived in a little world of your own. And it was a world within which you were very important: you were at its centre. When you needed attention, you bawled for it, and it usually came running! This was your truly human spiritual level during your life on earth. But this innocently self-centred state did not last very long before your brain began to develop and understand something of your world, your eyes started to look around more keenly and observe your surroundings. You quickly learnt to appreciate your own family, and more slowly you learnt about your own limitations, your own place in the world. This was your animal spiritual level; think back to your pre-teen years – you were a little animal, were you not? Sometimes wild, sometimes kittenish.

As you approached your teens you would have become a little more aggressive, a little more inclined to assert yourself in an arrogant manner, quick to put other people in their place – in short your classroom at school was a competitive place, and wherever you hung out with other kids, that was a bit of a battlefield too. This was your 'plant' spiritual level, striving for your own place in the sun. Then, as your teenage years set in, you became more interested in getting hold of some spending money rather than merely throwing your weight around; and as you became a young adult your interests were centred on *things* — holding down a job perhaps, making a living. This meant that you had gained the 'material' level. Some individuals go on from there to achieve quite amazing things: to become rich and famous, empire-builders, or brilliant scientists. This easy-getting stage is what I call 'the light of the material', because it contains a certain sort of spiritual enlightenment — on the material plane. It is also called 'the fall of the Archangel Lucifer'.

The case is similar with the whole human race seen as an entity — or equally with separate civilisations. They started off as a tribal society, probably simple hunter-gatherers. They were truly human, but humans without clothes or tools or weapons are very helpless creatures: naked and defenceless against extreme weather and against the teeth and claws of nature. But blessed with the marvellous human brain, people soon learnt how to build shelters, to make clothes to keep them warm, to make weapons and tools. This is quite unlike the beasts, which can function only within their own narrow instinctually-appointed limits. Humans watched how nature worked and learnt from it; they observed all the animals and plants, thought about them, and wondered how they could use them, experimenting with this method and that until they achieved what they felt they needed. This was the crux of the original 'human instinct': the capacity to observe, to see how everything worked and make best use of it. It is quite understandable that the people would have felt superior — godlike — realising that they could lord it over the world and sit in judgment over nature as they saw fit.

Then in later times the people, or the members of some particular race or civilisation, having quite inadvertently adopted some of the instincts of the beasts in the quest to make their own lives more comfortable, started to behave something like animals themselves, setting out their own territories, marking, expanding and guarding them, introducing new patterns of behaviour, exploiting the animal world by farming instead of hunting. Occasionally they would stage raids on neighbouring tribes and their lands, and capture animals and people as though they too were animals. Some races became very bold and invaded neighbouring lands one after another to create empires, taking over the reins of government for themselves.

Later still, people began to feel that they, as individuals, wanted a larger or more personal share of the world. Their territorial claims became fiercer and more ruthless. Power seemed all-important at that time, and they were often inspired to make war on other races, or even neighbouring branches of their own race. They had acquired something of the instincts of the plants which are obliged to battle for their right to live, even at the expense of others. Time-lapse photography of a woodland thicket will clearly show how every member or each species within the community tries to overpower the others, to smother their individuality, and to take over their piece of land.

Later again the people, the race, or the civilisation quite suddenly will begin to make progress in the material sphere. A sudden surge of new industrial inventions will change their lives for ever. They become able to travel much more freely, to work much more efficiently, and to accomplish a whole variety of things that would have been impossible before. Industrial Revolutions change the face of their world, and set an unprecedented standard of luxurious living for those who find themselves in tune with this new spiritual level, exploitation and oppression for those who do not. This kind of class division becomes the order of the day. But by and large the standard of living rises in quite dramatic fashion, and everyday possessions proliferate. This, of course, constitutes the 'age of materiality': humans have descended into what some have called the realm of Satan. And from amongst these 'material' people, some individuals, or even whole nations, seem to advance more than the rest, shining brightly and proudly in their success, effortlessly, it seems, acquiring more and more possessions, more money, more new inventions. These few have reached what I call the light of the material – the archangelic light zone which forms the translucent but impenetrable roof of materiality.

Great religions of the world also undergo much the same process, a similar decline taking place through the various 'levels' of nature, and simple observation of time scales will show this decline taking place in historical terms. A world religion starts high, in the spiritual realms above the normal human level, and at first the followers of a new religion are orientated towards that high ideal, towards the purity of spirit. But as more people embrace it, the body of the religion begins to sink to the ordinary 'human' level. This is when human cleverness enters a religion and takes it over, trying to make sense of it. Instead of merely accepting its spiritual influence and living up to it submissively, its adherents begin to theorise, to add bits of their own philosophies, their own sense of morality, glossing over the parts they find difficult to understand, trying to rationalise what should be an abstract, spiritual matter – dumbing it down perhaps, so that their human brains can encompass it. This is the time when little stories are invented to explain any phenomena which seem to be miraculous and put these things in terms that the common people – still orientated towards the old gods and goddesses of nature – can accept. True spirituality on earth often looks too 'normal' to be believable, and any kind of 'spiritual' manifestation has to appear unearthly and supernatural in order for it to be accepted.

Later on the religious body reaches the 'animal' phase: an expansive period during which its adherents set out to spread its boundaries, extolling it for its wisdom and virtue and cleverness: this is the preaching, evangelising stage by means of which a religion is able to extend its influence, albeit its humanised, or should we say 'animalised' form of influence. Later still, the body of a religion reaches its 'plant' level – the emotionally fierce and fanatical level during which its adherents are easily roused to anger and aggression, even going so far as to believe that this arrogant 'plant nature' is the true nature of their religion. During this stage of decline people may think nothing of oppressing or even killing others in the name of their religion, and are liable to stage holy wars, crusades or jihads to spread their roots and tendrils ever wider.

Later again the 'material' stage of a world religion sets in, and its adherents will thankfully have lost their arrogance and become much more amenable to other ways and tolerant of other beliefs. This of course is largely because they are behaving in the manner of 'things' – certainly content to let their religion stay within its own bounds, apparently faithful to their principles, but by the laws of materiality their religious feelings can readily become orientated towards the sentimental and intellectual aspects instead of the original high spiritual basis. People within this material level of religion will still retain all the other levels within their own inner selves, and depending upon circumstances, are able to call upon their plant-soul, their animal-soul, or their human-soul, as well as the powerful material-soul, to give them the broadest possible gamut of possibilities.

Many people have wondered why a religion that seems to have been based on love, tolerance and understanding can possibly condone violence and cruelty, and whichever religion you have in mind, the record and the reason will be very similar. Religious development runs parallel with the spiritual development of the people who embrace it, and inevitably there comes a time in religious history when aggressive defensiveness comes to the fore. The adherents of that religion will certainly not see it in those terms; they will be genuinely affronted, filled with fervour and righteous indignation. Think in terms of centuries. Because they are religious people, and because both they and their religion have descended from their original high spiritual level and arrived at the level of plant-force instincts, those who have communally reached the level of plants will sense that the realm of Satan (that is, the

SUBTLE MATERIALITY

level of the material life-forces) is just below them. Seeing this as the ultimate evil, they will resist the final descent, and consider those other peoples and religions that have made this descent to be satanic. But without this descent, without embracing the material forces of spirituality in their own innermost being, they cannot experience compassion. Spiritual love, tolerance and mercy will remain empty words. An even balance of all these spiritual levels is essential for these compassionate qualities to operate, because they depend upon an even combination of *all* passions, and not merely selected ones.

A few individuals within any world religion may later go on to reach 'the light of the material'. In this context it is a condition which allows them to recapture or re-experience something of its former glory, something of the wonder of true spirituality – while still encased within the satanic realm, the zone of materiality. When this happens, such people are liable to become engrossed in the seemingly miraculous supernatural experiences to be found in that strange zone. They may become 'holy men' or 'holy women', believing themselves to be spiritually adept, and attract followers eager to hang on to their every word. Or, and best of all, they may be inspired to begin the long trek back up the wilderness trail, to join the flow of creation, and finally to re-attain that spiritual perfection which their religion has lost over the centuries.

The material life force is the spiritual force of the physical world itself. We are all 'tuned in' to it, because we and all living creatures are already part of it. Our whole physical being is founded upon it and we draw our energy from it, from whichever direction that energy may *appear* to be channelled. Without the material life force we would all cease to exist. Certainly there is a subtle or supernatural essence within materiality, but the material world is a world of passion, of pulling away from spirit. Spirituality within the material life force is what we mean when we speak of 'the occult', and almost by definition success or progress in the occult sphere is directly opposed to spiritual progress. This should be clearly understood by prospective witches or wizards. There is nothing within the material zone that can lift the soul to a higher level, or put our divided souls in touch with spirit, but there is a great deal that will make it *feel* that way. The deeper we delve into what we consider to be the mysterious nature of materiality, the more we explore the light zone of the Archangel Lucifer, the deeper into the underworld will our inner selves be lured.

It may seem obvious, but it is worth saying: *things* cannot be holy; *places* cannot be holy. They may induce feelings of awe – a magnificent cathedral may well do that – or an emotional feeling of peace. They may induce a sense of mystery, or a yearning for some kind of lost values, as a prehistoric monument may well do – but this is all in the mind. There are systems intended to organise the elements, manipulate the material; whole industries have grown up based on the art of moving things around, re-orientating objects, counting things up, consulting this or that, and there is little to choose between them. The supernatural element in cases such as these lies within your own material-soul. Your own inner self is probably not connected with your thought processes, though it may well be able to inform you of almost anything you need to know, if it had the means. If any of the material systems of divination (a pack of cards, shall we say) seems to be working for you, it will be because your own inner self is providing the information by way of symbols on the material plane.

It all comes back to the age-old exhortation to 'know thyself'. The material life force is very powerful and holds everything together. If you willingly allow your own soul to become so heavy, so engrossed in the vibrations of this force that it 'dances to the same tune', then, like physical matter, it is liable to be drawn down and held by the force of gravity. Like a ghost in chains, you will have made an unpleasant little hell for yourself.

All passions, we could say, are 'bad' in the sense that they strengthen the material parts of us, mind and body, at the expense of the spiritual part – the soul as it could be. But they are 'good' in the sense that they keep you in bodily health and give you the drive to succeed in worldly pursuits: work, sport and so on. But we could equally say that there is one 'good' passion in the spiritual sense, and this is the passion of faith, representing the highest point, the pinnacle of the material life force. This is the quiet passion that urges you to seek a way to climb back, to try to regain your lost innocence, even to unite with long-forgotten spirit. But even this passion is 'bad' in the worldly sense that it is not going to help you to achieve wealth or material success in the normal course of events. To be effective this faith will be directed away from the material zone and towards the innocence of childhood. You may of course apply faith here and there, to this and that, to the paranormal, to crystals, to religious icons, to holy books, or anything else, but all these things are 'material', and the material plane should not be the final resting place of faith; it is really being wasted on materiality.

I have mentioned the 'light of the material' in its religious context, and of course some people find their way to this magical zone in the secular context too: they become rather like King Solomon in all his glory, representing the pinnacle of material light power. Such people are at the top of their tree, full of cleverness and skill at succeeding in whatever they want to do. They have the energy and aptitude to put any enterprise into operation, direct it and cream off the profits. The material forces of course are the source of energy and wealth on earth, so such a person is never likely to go short of these things — until death finally puts an end to it. But even death may carry you into this light zone. You can even enter it on a physical basis (if only briefly) when your body is put through some kind of gravitational stress. People who have experienced 'near-death' have often reported something of this nature: a blissful zone of light into which they entered. Plainly this magical zone is to be approached by way of the material forces of the earth. It is ironic that those attaining the intellectual 'light' are invariably convinced that they have risen or climbed there, when it would be more accurate to say that they have sunk to what is in fact the very fundament of materiality itself.

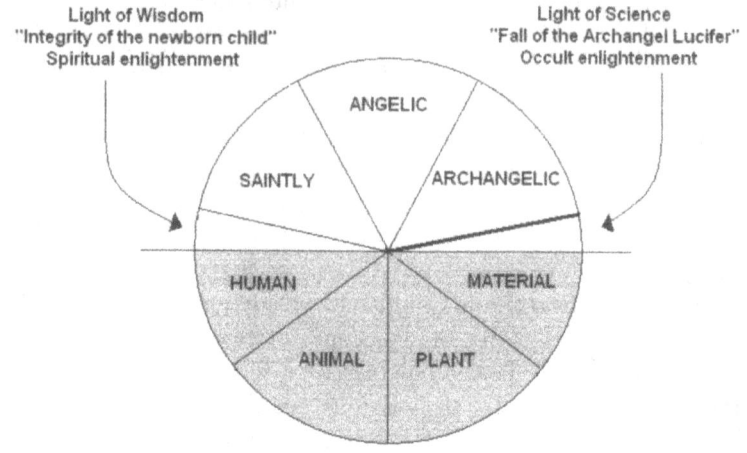

In my view, nothing explains this whole process so clearly and simply as the 'world mandala' above. Human ambitions in the first place lead us out of our own birthright, our own human zone, down the *passionate* path, through the animal and then the plant zones. From then on the push towards material success may *seem* like an uphill struggle, a climb towards the light, even though our broad objective view tells us that it must involve a further and ever more drastic descent. All this happens on the level of the soul, of course, and our brains, our hearts and minds, our ego, will probably entertain a very different overall view of what is happening. We are unable to see it at the time, for the simple reason that our brains are not normally in contact with our souls. Our brains (or our hearts – our emotions) like to think that they alone are the wise and important ones. Establishing or re-establishing a spiritual contact enabling our brains to be in touch with our souls would seem an important issue to be faced, but amazingly few people care to face it. If the zone of materiality is 'the broad and bright highway' it is because the passions accompany those who walk along it. The lonely 'straight and narrow path' leading back through the realms of plants and animals to the human zone, is not an overly moral or sanction-ridden path:

it is lonely because it is free from passions. The light of the material is an exciting place, and the road there is bound to be thronged. The path to wholeness, being free of passions, is comparatively boring and can never be popular. This is the point where the 'good passion' of faith comes into play. Christians will recall the assurance: 'Seek and ye shall find. Knock and it shall be opened unto you'. No guarantees; it is all a matter of faith.

Creating a balance

All the vibrations of nature are given their energy by the powerhouse of the material force, and to this extent all life forms are under the control of this power. Humans alone have the will to force the pace, to wish to acquire more, and they alone in nature are able to manipulate and make good use of materiality. Animals have an animal-soul; plants have a plant-soul; materials have a material-soul. But humans have a human-soul, and also an animal-soul, a plant-soul, and a material-soul. Without this variety it would be impossible for us to play the great snakes-and-ladders game of life. So think of yourself as having four souls or, if you prefer, four distinct divisions of your soul, each one particularly sensitive to a distinct level of influence, and operative within that level. Suppose your human-soul were very powerful and the others weak, you would be an uncivilised and primitive person. We have already noted what happens when the animal-soul dominates, and experienced the dangerous fanaticism that ensues when the plant-soul is the most powerful. Our main problem in the west is that we are in danger of strengthening our material-soul out of proportion to the others.

If the first rule of common sense is to 'know yourself', the second common sense rule should be: 'allow yourself to be in balance'. This is an issue that must be faced by all who wish to know more about their own selves, and the possibility of finding a spiritual path. The four souls represent the seat of the passions within the human condition, each with its own distinctive flavour. But when these four are in perfect balance, all the passions will be working equally together to create 'compassion'. The four soul divisions will then become united in one all-loving soul able to apply whatever passion may be required to meet any circumstance, and apply it with the backing of spiritually inspired love; and that can't be bad.

CHAPTER ELEVEN

The Goddess Within

ACCORDING to the biblical Book of Genesis, man came first. Masculinity, it says, was created before femininity. The archetypal male principle seems firmly rooted at least in that particular story of creation. There are other creation myths which see the creative principle as basically female, but in the Judeo-Christian-Moslem tradition, the man Adam was made by God the Creator, in his own image. For so basic a principle to be seen as wholly male is plainly biased. As a foundation on which we all have to stand it can be felt as a sore point for some people even today – that feminine qualities should have developed apparently as an afterthought to balance sheerly one-sided masculinity. Mother earth, after all, is not usually thought of as father earth. In its favour, however, is the equally plain fact that the man – masculinity – can be seen as a channel, whereas the woman – femininity – can be seen as a vessel in which to receive whatever is channelled, and then to blend it, modify it, and reproduce it in a new form.

Femininity, it could be said, in modifying what has been transmitted, reduces laws to rules. Looked at in a personal sense, if the male-god principle, in its functioning, is to be regarded as judgmental and impersonal, immutable, not to be swayed by force or even reason, it follows that pristine femininity, in modifying that judgment, should be conciliatory, mediatory, intercessional, protective, and altogether more personal and intimate. Intolerance, if it is to be moved at all, can only be moved or checked by love working towards compassion. Main line evolution functions on impersonal material balance, and personal spiritual balance is essential for love to operate.

It is the female principle of providing that balancing force that shows itself able to live in both worlds, heavenly and earthly, able to exert influence over the elemental powers both above and below, as well as the people in between. In this context the combined goddesses of old provided an abstract influence, fearlessly submissive, submissively fearless, which, seen from the petitioner's point of view, seemed to rise and fall and rise again; to initiate a regular cycle – the cycle of nature from the human viewpoint. The only kind of influence capable of swaying the dominating maleness of otherwise immutable heavenly laws was the faculty of fearless submission tempered with the art of manipulation. If it could be called a power in its own right, it was the submissive power of faith which, we are told, can move mountains.

It is axiomatic that femininity, if it is to function effectively (and I mean in real life here on earth), should never dominate. Even today, a domineering woman with undisputed power and command tends to be disliked even by ardent feminists, who despise her as a make-believe man. Femininity has to involve the art of persuasion rather than coercion. Neither prayer not petition, if it is to be carried aloft, can be propelled forcibly to its target; it can only be wafted gently by way of the female principle of submissive intercession. Empowerment on earth however, the putting into practice of the results of that intercession, perceiving the outcome and putting it to practical use, as I see it, is best effected by way of the male principle.

Paradoxical it may seem, but the *inner self* of man as well as woman must be seen as feminine when pitting itself against the unremitting maleness of the universal principle of power. To God, as a channel of 'will', the soul of man has to be receptively female by nature. The vehicle of intercession may itself be male, but the innate quality of femininity directs the progress of that vehicle. The spirituality of masculine man, though not at all effeminate, nevertheless embodies an element of femininity able to exert, not force or power, but a gently moulding influence, working to modify principles and laws that are all too readily seen as dogmatic and unbending.

THE GODDESS WITHIN

It is a balance working towards wholeness. Love from the masculine viewpoint can be symbolised in many ways. There is the earthy human love represented by the male Eros, or Cupid, and the even more earthy human-beast-plant love symbolised by Bacchus Dionysus and Priapus; between them, they ensure a well-stocked earth. Earthy love, we could say, takes place at the feet of the nature goddess. As we move higher, away from her feet, into the rarefied atmosphere of Olympus, the loving instinct too becomes rarefied, sublimated in the child self. The process can be seen in the story of Hebe, admired in ancient times by both Greeks and Romans as the much-coveted goddess of eternal youth, who acted as hand-maiden or cup-bearer to the gods. She was thought able to restore the vigour of youth to mortal men as they aged – this was the vulgar view – and, through intercession, to free oppressed people from both their earthly and their spiritual bonds and chains. But subsequently she was replaced by Ganymede, the handsome youth abducted by Zeus – the principle of feminine intercession at work within the essence of masculinity.

On a similar theme there are ancient myths which involved the castration of a god, sometimes in revenge by his own children for being too unyielding – by Cronus with his sickle, in the case of his father, the eccentric old fertility god Uranus. Symbolically, the act of emasculation opens the way for new birth of the female principle, as the emergence of Venus Aphrodite from the foam stirred up in the sea by the fallen severed parts of Uranus: Venus, epitome of female beauty, but who could also display hermaphroditic characteristics when circumstances seemed to require it. The life principle which is normally stored above the earth becomes available below. When the god is symbolically emasculated – or emasculates himself like Attis beneath the pine tree – this is to enable him to act as go-between, to intercede by way of natural laws with the fundamentally masculine forces which may otherwise overlook human needs. The blood, or passion, of Attis's lost manhood flowed into mother earth, trapping the life principle beneath the ground, where it stays captive and dormant until able to give rise to the flowers of spring – in his case the violet, symbol of faith, innocence and modesty.

Literal minds in the past have often taken a step too far, putting into practice a principle only half-way understood. In classical times, like the priest-servants of the heavenly queen before them, the human priests of Diana Artemis, of Astarte, Ashtoreth and Atargatis, were obliged to castrate themselves too. If nothing else, it was an acknowledgment that the channelling power of masculinity could have no legitimate role to play in the intercessional process over which they were intended to preside. Fruitfulness, by way of myth, depends on the loss of masculinity, in the same way that rebirth, in one sense or another, is conditional upon death. Think of the cycle of nature and the principle of reincarnation as it applies to plants and its relevance to the human condition, to the possibility of rebirth: 'a grain of wheat remains a solitary grain unless it falls into the ground and dies; but if it dies, it bears a rich harvest'. This is the non-mythical principle of Christianity at work: 'Sown in the earth as a perishable thing, it is raised imperishable.'

Awareness of spirituality, its practical experience, creates a female principle of intercession which can grow into something vastly substantial. In ancient times we might have called this understanding the intercession of Venus Aphrodite, or Diana Artemis, or Astarte, or even mother earth. The intercessory goddess has her feet in the world of nature, her head in the heavens, remonstrating with the elements, charming the gods and manipulating the fates in a way which could never have been achieved by force. But of course there is no need now to invent modern versions of ancient goddesses: men as well as women can find the goddess in themselves by leaving the spiritual channel open, and functioning as a vessel, to receive. This is the ultimate 'tuning in' to natural vibrations: the finest, highest and most subtle, most diffuse vibration to be found in nature. If you can find this quietly submissive dimension within your own self, imbibing in silence by allowing thoughts and feelings to subside in full consciousness, your own path of intercession will be cleared and made straight, for the gateway to that path is already there within your own self: your own soul.

THE GODDESS WITHIN

Vibrations of the Inner Self

I have already mentioned how it is that our prayers, if answered, will necessarily have been heard by the higher parts of our own self, for it is only by way of these higher parts of the whole self that anything can be done in the realm of the miraculous. The greatest characteristic of a real goddess, one who encompasses the whole of nature, will be that she is able to apply compassion to a situation; and compassion, or love, is greater than hope, greater even than faith. Without compassion, without this broad type of love, we are necessarily incomplete. Even the greatest prophets of old — shall we say Abraham, who lived in the days when people were still purely 'human', or Moses, who lived when people were still 'human-animal' — seemed to possess not so much as a shred of compassion; their stories make this abundantly clear. Their higher human passions were certainly powerful qualities, but their lower passions, the qualities of their plant and material natures, were weak.

People today tend towards the opposite case: their lowest, material passion is powerful, their higher passions progressively weaker, from the plant through the animal and up to the original human level. What is lacking in us is the even balance of passions that together make up the quality of compassion. Where the material or 'satanic' force is weak in a person, they are unlikely to be devoted to anything with solidity, and this certainly includes other people; we are all solid objects. The material passion is indeed an essential part of the soul of a well-rounded person.

The important point is that true compassion, or 'spiritual love', can happen only when the passions are evenly balanced: anything less produces only misleadingly false compassion — a compassion that goes 'so far and no further'. True compassion will include 'warts and all', bad as well as good, the spontaneous act of feeling everything that is to be felt about a person, or a thing, or a situation. If your own balance excludes the human passion, for instance, it may manifest itself as a compassion that is directed towards animals but not towards humans. Or if your balance proves to be powerful in the material and plant sections, extending upwards only enough to include the plant level, you may have 'a passion for flowers'. Perhaps we could say that having 'green fingers' is an expression of compassion towards plants. And if your balance extends upwards only enough to cover the material force, you may have a passion for certain material objects – not necessarily a love of money, but a real love for certain categories of things, in the familiar way that so many enthusiasts, experts and hobbyists do have.

As civilised human beings most of us strive towards a modicum of worldly success – indeed, it has often been said that we have a duty to provide for our own life, and for the lives of any dependants we may have. But 'you can't take it with you', and we also have an obligation towards our inner lives, and the inner welfare of our dependants too. It would seem fairly obvious that we need to achieve a balance within ourselves, simply in order to fulfil these dual duties. Our life's journey, it has truthfully been said, should be 'from the spiritual (the point of birth and the origins of our soul) to the material, and back to the spiritual again'. And as somebody else once said, 'we are all being carried on a journey through life, and we might as well do something useful to pass the time'. What better provision could we make than to 'get it all together' and try to balance ourselves out?

In fact, and in practice, it would probably prove impossible for anyone to achieve this through their own volition, by their own will-power, though goodness knows a great many have tried it. It can however happen of its own accord, by degrees, when we decide to take the return half of that journey; never forget that the highest or purest passion of the material realm is 'faith'. As far as I am aware, there is only one way to let this happen, to bring the passions that have filled our souls into balance and commence the climb back to truly human status and the world of spirit that lies beyond – while at the same time pursuing our everyday lives of learning and earning. It sounds simple enough, but in fact it must be the greatest challenge any of us can face. It means allowing the soul to be laid open so as to pave the way for the entry of spirit; to feel the vibrations of life by way of our own soul, our own inner self, when it has been stirred into wakefulness. Only by this means can we begin the climb back through the coarse influences of nature, throwing out the now unwanted passions as we go, layer by layer. It will certainly be the journey of a lifetime, and it will last to the end of your life and probably beyond – and your dependants (and perhaps even your ancestors) will feel the benefit as well.

(I recommend to you the way called *Subud*. This is just a name, obviously, and there may be other ways which lead to the same results, but I have not heard of them. It is not a method or a teaching or a kind of religion; it simply helps your soul to be open, temporarily laying aside the passions, and everything that subsequently happens to you is happening within yourself. It is not a way of 'doing', or 'thinking', or 'feeling', or believing this or that: it simply allows the process to begin).

So this, more or less, is how it all works. All these 'influences', all these 'levels', all these passions, vibrations, strange experiences, are all part of your own self. Above you is the channel; your own conscious awareness is the vessel. If you can visualise the course of your life as a ladder, or perhaps a column, or even a well-shaft down which we have all had the misfortune to slide, you will see that we really need to continue the descent within this shaft of life until we reach rock bottom. We have no choice; it is only the hard base of ultimate materiality that will lend us a point of leverage, a firm ladder base from which to begin the ascent – our return journey. Your personal impetus comes, when the way is clear, from non-personal spirit, as when the rays of the sun may shine briefly down the shaft. The idea often 'comes to light' when prehistoric buildings are being discussed, from Stone Age caves to megalithic tombs or chambers, from Stonehenge to the pyramids. It is a theme archaeologists are fond of exploring: prehistoric people believed this, or believed that, and oriented their structures according to the changing patterns of the sky.

Actually, the essence of ideas such as these comes not from the ancient stones themselves, but from the inner selves of the people exploring them. The sun, of course, symbolises the spirit without which there would be no life. Whether they acknowledge it or not, people who take an interest in what happens when a ray of sunlight works its magic and hits the spot on midsummer's morn, or whenever it may be – are looking for a way to understand the spiritual forces of materiality, trying to crack those secrets. When their conscious attention is diverted from the outer to the inner dimension, they might just possibly be able to experience the truth of these things, inwardly, for themselves.

There is no need to possess acute brains or degrees in this or that in order to unravel the mystery, and actually travel up that ray of light on the inner plane yourself. All you need is that uppermost passion of the material soul level – the 'good passion' of faith, plus a little help, perhaps, from your fellow spiritual travellers. 'Seek and ye shall find!' If you do put this suggestion into practice, your first 'spiritual' experiences will necessarily be of a 'material' nature. When the process of uncovering your soul begins to penetrate, you may find that you have been carried, albeit briefly, into that magical zone of the 'light of the material' where, if you are at all sensitive to spiritual matters, you may experience all sorts of miraculous things. But as you are now in possession of the greater picture, you will not want to remain there: treat it as a mere foretaste of better things to come. This zone of light is certainly the goal of occultists and wizards and so forth, but it is still situated within the ultimate depths of materiality. If you really do remain there, like Merlin the Magician you may end up trapped inside the rock. It is still symbolic, of course, but it is not just nonsense, and I think we should be heedful of it.

As you have slid down the well-shaft of life, as I say, you need to reach the base of the material before you can effectively start to climb. At this point your personal 'material-soul', having come to awareness, may well take on a separate life of its own, helping and advising, as befits your 'soul-brother' or 'soul-sister', as

THE GODDESS WITHIN

the case might be. But as these contents are your own, your material-soul is capable of misleading as well as advising you. Some people, having started along this way and experiencing something like this which seems truly amazing, assume that they have already 'arrived', already regained the truly human level from which they started life, or that they have become 'spiritually adept'. Don't fall for it! The lure of materiality is all the greater, all the more enhanced, once you have experienced something of the magical light zone. Watch what happens with interest; don't fight it, but don't hang on to it either; let it go when the time comes. You are still on the bottom rung of the ladder. The penetrating sunlight swiftly moves on, and the dark well-shaft still looms above you!

As your material-soul is left behind, you may seem to have lost strength and sense of purpose. The well-shaft, don't forget, is you, your own life, and the 'souls' or essences of these levels of being are still your own, eventually to be reunited, atoned. The highest passion of the material level is 'faith', and faith was needed for the process to begin. We spoke of the 'human-plant' level of spirituality, the stage to be reached as you leave the material level behind, and with it the confidential advice and help of your 'material-soul'. Your 'plant-soul' cannot offer much in the way of material advice, but the highest passion of the plant level of spirituality is 'patience', and patience will certainly be needed during this dull, dark, emotional but seemingly spiritually barren part of your climb. Above the plants are the beasts, and your 'animal-soul' will guide you along this part of your climb. The highest passion of the animal level is 'submission', and this is where the goddess within will be of the utmost help – fearlessly submissive and submissively fearless, she will see you through. Nearing the top of your well-shaft the human life forces will help you up towards the light. The highest passion of the human level is 'sincerity', and it is sincerity of purpose that will help you reach the point at which the passions can begin to combine to produce 'compassion', the spiritual love which is the characteristic sign of a whole person; the person who has been to a certain extent made whole; the person, in fact, who can come to appreciate that 'God is love'.

CHAPTER TWELVE

Transcending Nature

TO RECAPITULATE the most important points that have been covered so far, we could say:

A   There are two ways of looking at what we might call our spiritual origin: firstly the evolution of the entire human race from the state symbolised by the Garden of Eden; secondly our personal evolution from the innocent beginnings of babyhood.

B   Our susceptibility to the vibrations of nature which are all around us has caused our spiritual centre of gravity to decline throughout our own personal lives, as well as throughout the lives and history of humanity as a whole.

C   Our essential soul quality has passed through the life force originally intended for humans, through the life forces intended for the animals, through the life forces intended for plants, and down into the life forces intended for the minerals, rocks and material objects. This last life force forms the spiritual centre of gravity for the great majority of people, good and bad.

D   On the way down from our long-lost spiritual status, we have learnt to appreciate the beauty of our environment; we have taken in the peaceful influence of the rising sun; the emotional and physical balance of the moon; we have admired the dawn and marvelled at the heavens, and even ascribed to the planets a reflection of our own human psyche.

E   We have recognised our emotions for what they are, and learnt to distinguish them from the power of reason on the one hand, and the power of faith on the other.

TRANSCENDING NATURE

F   We have acquired some inkling of the nature of 'passion', and see it as the factor which draws the soul downwards towards the material level, rather than up towards the spiritual realm.

G   We have at last realised that the expressions of spiritual power that have been shown us by way of our religions can never be more than a symbol of that power, but that such symbols have been and still are helpful in allowing us to see where we stand in the order of life.

H   We have taken to heart the often unsuspected fact that the vibrations of nature really do affect our lives and need to be respected.

I   We have learnt to enjoy the world of nature and marvel at its beauty and complexity, and have discovered how to tune in to its complex vibrations without becoming further enslaved by them.

J   We have learnt the wisdom of stewardship – of protecting all life forms that share our planet, and have seen some of the misfortunes that can result from directing our passions towards them inappropriately.

K   We appreciate that the free and healthy cycle of nature is essential for the well-being of our planet, and that we should do all we can to help it along, without finding ourselves caught up in it and ruled by it.

L   We have seen for ourselves how the practice of wasting or abusing any aspect of nature can backfire on our human well-being, and be the cause of hardship.

M   we acknowledge that it is no bad thing to seek out our innermost feelings, whether we do this by enhancing our understanding and enjoyment of nature, by meditation, or by any other means.

N   One of our most abiding pieces of wisdom expresses our need to 'know ourselves' without our habitual disguises.

O   Many contradictory statements have been made by religious people concerning what they consider to be 'God's will'. But we have to learn that it is God's will for us to descend into the spiritual depths of materiality, before being able to rise to the spiritual heights.

P   We have discovered that spiritual love, or compassion, requires an even blend of all the passions available to us, including the material or so-called 'satanic' passions.

Q   Reason is telling us that we should encourage the submissive side of our nature in order to submit to higher spiritual forces when they make their presence known. In no way can spiritual submission be correctly interpreted as weakness.

R   Spiritual power belongs to God. The human will to power and the acquisition of spirituality are incompatible.

S   It is through our experience of the material life force – the lowest and coarsest of the spiritual life forces – that we can discover that the positive side of desire or greed is 'faith'.

T   From our experience of the plant life force, we can discover that the positive side of arrogance and ferocity is 'patience'.

U   From our experience of the animal life force, we can discover that the positive side of pride and self-satisfaction is 'submission'.

V   From our experience of the human life force, we can discover that the positive side of egotism and conceit is 'sincerity' – a willingness to acknowledge and discard, as far as possible, our own less desirable characteristics.

W   Having travelled as it were, on the level of soul, from the spiritual to the material, some of us have seen a need to travel back to the spiritual state again, carrying with us, as far as possible, the benefits of materiality – our civilisation and culture.

X   If there are vibrations of a finer quality than those of nature which we have already experienced, it seems plain that by intention and willpower alone we are unable to locate them. We reach the conclusion that we need to find some practical means, not dependent upon our desires, whereby we can receive truly spiritual vibrations and make our return journey possible.

Y   If we are fortunate enough to find the way and set out along it, we will find too that only faith can provide the impetus; only patience can enable it to happen; only submission to higher powers will ensure our progress; only sincerity in letting go of our faults when the time comes, will finally lead to the restoration of our rightful place in the spiritual hierarchy.

Z   Divinity is not to be found in books or beliefs or special places. Divinity or closeness to God can be approached only one way – through our own inner self when the vibrations of nature, via the workings of our everyday hearts and minds, are stilled. In the words of the psalm, 'Be still and know that I am God'. People of any religion or none stand equal in this. It is only through our own self that we can approach the highest; you will not 'find God' outside of yourself.

Vibrations of the Inner Self

It has been called the fall from grace, the mythological expulsion from the Garden of Eden, the spiritual descent from a saintly high-human status above and overlooking the whole of nature, a state of submission towards that which we have called 'the father figure'. It is this pristine state of submission, this original subtle variation of the higher human 'instincts' working through what we call 'the inner self', that remains to be regained. Only then can the human life cycle approach completion or, as some might say, perfection. The perfect human life cycle may best be summed up in the words of Muhammad Subuh Sumohadiwidjojo: 'A journey from the spiritual to the material, and back again to spirit'.

It is not really something we can 'do', because the operative factor is 'submitting' rather than 'doing'. It has been said: 'Man does not choose; spirit chooses'. Only God can say who or what or when or if. We can only prepare ourselves and declare ourselves ready and willing to submit, and the best way in which we can prepare ourselves is by finding some person or people who are already on this path, and who may be able and willing to act as intermediaries, catalysts in a process which may set your own receiving in motion. And 'When two or three are gathered together...' and everything proceeds according to expectations, sooner or later you will feel these vibrations which rise apparently from deep within your own being. They will – again, sooner or later – result in involuntary movements and possibly vocal sounds to which you should submit, following the movements and voicing the utterances.

This will comprise the beginnings of a spiritual exercise: the movements and sounds are not prompted by your brain, not from your intentions, your thoughts or emotions. Your own familiar processes of thinking and feeling will stand aside and act as mere observers, watching and listening to whatever occurs. They must not take part themselves; auto-suggestion should not enter into it. Neither must you allow yourself to fall into some kind of trance-state. Everything about you must be fully aware, fully conscious. Similar sounds and movements may well result from trance-states, but these arise from the material life forces flavoured with the essence of plants and animals. Spiritualist mediums may fall into a trance-state, and they may well contact shades of the dead; but there is no such thing as a *spiritual* trance. Whatever else it may do, 'spiritualism' cannot contact spirit, and this is a point well worth remembering.

Do not be misled. In the normal course of life many people

receive all sorts of apparently alien thoughts and disembodied voices produced as a result, perhaps, of what is known as ESP. I know that when somebody thinks a critical thought directed at me (whenever I am least expecting it), that thought arises in my brain word for word, though it seems to arise from some part of the hindbrain rather than the forebrain usually associated with the thought processes. This always seems mysterious, psychic even, but it is not 'spiritual'. It is not at all the same thing as 'receiving' during the spiritual exercise. The sounds you utter will not 'arise' inside your brain in this way; along with the movements you receive and follow they will be spontaneous and unheralded. Your movements and utterances will seem to possess varying qualities: they will not necessarily be pious or prayerful; they may just as likely be profane or even shocking. They are not at all the same as the 'charismatic' movements and utterances triggered by the emotional feelings. They are not 'prayers': they are your own innermost contents being cleaned out. Ultimately, only experience will show you the real difference; all you have to do is to remain wide awake but with your mind relaxed, and submit to the process with sincerity, whether sounds and movements are being experienced by you or not.

Your movements in the spiritual exercise may be accompanied by strange smells which certainly do not arise from nature. Some of these may seem like incense, others may seem foul. Either occur because material passions are being dispelled, and this ethereal smell is one of their properties. You may discover that the original 'incense' is (or was) the smell of departing evil spirits, rather then 'the odour of sanctity', but it shows that 'holiness' is present during the process of disturbing and releasing these characteristics. Perhaps at one time these things were part of the common experience, when the 'Garden of Eden' was still a meaningful concept. At all events, artificial, 'material' incense was developed over the ages, using resin and various other plant materials which were burnt to represent the prayers of the people as these petitions were visualised ascending to heaven. This was of course an attempt to recapture that original incense when it had been retained only as a folk memory. But truly 'spiritual' smells, good or bad, remind us that the only truly meaningful form of prayer is a spiritual 'receiving', resulting in the long-term purification of soul-contents at the material level − on the level, that is, of nature.

True submission in the context of the spiritual exercise constitutes the reality of prayer, and only prayer of that calibre can be sure of actually reaching its target. Everyday religious prayers which stem at least partially from the passions, the desires, the emotions, cannot really be expected to penetrate the heaviness of materiality that normally surrounds us − the matrix of passions which we have acquired by reacting to the natural forces that have invaded our being. All such passions derive from the instincts of nature which are below the truly human spiritual level. Real prayers do not need words − all our needs are already known by the soul − and they certainly do not need desires: they depend only upon submission when the passions and desires are at rest. Only real prayers such as these are fine enough to penetrate the smothering layers that have cloaked what should be the highest part of our own selves, and thus reach their target.

It is only the coarse vibrations of the natural, physical world, expressed in our own passionate thoughts and feelings, that prevent us experiencing the spiritual vibrations of our own inner selves, linking us to a greater impersonal soul that seems to have lain dormant during much of our lives. Assisted by the presence of others who have already received this spiritual movement, spirit can enter the void left by your own stilling of thoughts and feelings, and by so doing stir the soul into wakefulness. It is not the spirit of this or that, not the various 'spirits of nature', but the real though utterly non-scientific Holy Spirit itself, which will enter you if you permit it. Through your own faith − the highest principle of the material life force; through your own patience − the highest principle of the plant life force; through your own submission − the highest principle of the animal life force; through your own sincerity − the highest principle of the human life force;

your soul will be set along the ultimate pilgrimage. These four qualities will combine to find the 'path that no fowl has seen', the path of which it was once said: 'Few there be who find it'. Even now at your point of entry you will already have gained the soul-state that holy men and women in the past may have achieved only after a lifetime of devotion. You will have received the inestimable boon of being able to start at the point which saints and sages, pious monks and sincere yogis can reach only by the end of their life, after many years of dedication, at their point of death.

If you are at all typical in that your own inner being has become immersed in the coarse life forces of materiality, when this path first becomes a reality, you may well seem to have been precipitated into a parallel world of occult wonders. This is because you are experiencing something of the 'light of the material'. These strange phenomena comprise the subtle side of solid materiality, and in your case they should be of a temporary nature. However marvellous your experiences may seem to be, they must be transcended. You will come to understand at first hand that you possess four personal 'souls' as well as the higher impersonal soul which can become filled with spirit. Your personal souls will have come to life, and they may become so real, so solid, so animated, that they can speak and act independently of your thoughts and feelings. They may offer you wise advice, or seemingly magical assistance. They may warn you of approaching danger, or point out things which you cannot see, or inform you of facts about which you were ignorant. But these four personal souls are motivated by the passions, loves and hates of nature; this is the nature of their contents. Marvellous though they undoubtedly are, as you progress along the spiritual path which you have gained, sooner or later you must be prepared to let them go.

The Way of Death

The spiritual path has been described as 'the way of death' because it depends upon the death of the passions. Normally it cannot be pursued before the physical death of the body, the heart with its emotions, the brain with its thoughts. Now we have access to the path, we find that it can be followed during our lifetime. It follows that the passions which in the past have sustained us while keeping us from the spiritual path, are the only part of us that must face death now. Our progress will depend largely upon our willingness to let these passions go when the time comes. Many aspirants remain on the lowest rung of 'Jacob's ladder', because of their unwillingness to do this. Your 'material soul' in particular, if it has become very powerful during your past life, may represent itself as your guide and mentor, quite independently of your thoughts, and pretend (or believe itself) to be some kind of high authority, holding you in its spell. This will be the first spiritual temptation that anyone has to encounter. Do not forget that the material life force, though so essential for material existence, represents the realm of Satan. Do not forget mythical stories about 'selling your soul to the devil'. Remember too that the highest and ultimately the most powerful passion within this material, satanic realm in which we all live is the passion of faith, and it will be faith that enables you to move on. At last you are in a position to rise above Satan, and by so doing to enter the spiritual territory of the Green Man.

If you accomplish this major step successfully, something of an anticlimax may set in. You may seem to have lost something precious. You may no longer experience magical happenings, occult smells, or the ability to see over horizons or into the future. Everyone's experiences will be different as we are all unique, but this tends to be the general pattern. Faith has carried you onto the next rung, and this is where the quality of patience will truly be needed. Material wealth and prestige are of course features of the material level of life, and you may find yourself losing out on some of these good things which previously you had taken for granted. At this point you will know for sure why the spiritual path can never be popular, why it will never win hearts and minds, why it will always remain a lonely, straight and narrow path standing in stark contrast with the brightly lit highway flanked with attractions of all sorts (some of which may be religious attractions), that leads in the opposite direction.

TRANSCENDING NATURE

During your progress over the years there may come back to you vivid memories of anything you may have done during your past life that may have caused harm or anguish, or suffering, or danger, or upset, or embarrassment to any person, and you will feel intense remorse for your wrong doings. Things of this nature, though they may have seemed well justified or even laudable at the time, you will now see as wholly wrong, and you will beg forgiveness. You will at last stand face to face with the 'mirror of karma' and understand that it is your own true self that stands in stern judgment of your own past misdeeds. All these things will come back to haunt and taunt you until you have fully atoned.

You will probably find that you no longer wish to pursue any activities that you have come to realise are in some way wrong, or contradictory to your own true nature. If you still do wrong you may find instant retribution in the form of misfortune in a measure equal to your own misdeeds. In fact, you should find that your whole life is balancing itself out, the past with the present, often in a startlingly practical way. For example you may have employed others in a menial capacity in the past, and you will now find that an equally menial way of life is thrust upon you for an equal period of time. This is purgatory in its true practical sense, the reality of atonement functioning while you live. Every participant on the spiritual path will have his or her own set of unique experiences, and it is all to the long-term good. You have to become balanced, the highest with the lowest, the best with the worst; rewards and punishments must equal themselves out; and all this happens during your everyday life.

The spiritual exercise itself is best practised on a regular basis, say for half an hour twice a week. Any more than this might be overdoing it. Obviously you need to retain all your normal mental and emotional control during daily life. If you find it too easy to 'let go' and overdo it, you may find yourself suffering something of a psychological or physical crisis. Old troubles, whether physical, emotional or mental, may come flooding back to plague you. Such things, or traces of them, will have been there all the time, hidden within your inner self; you have uncovered them and let them out. They need to go, of course, but take it easy! And once they have gone, take care not to invite them back again through the old habits of thinking.

Excessively intellectual or particularly clever people may see nothing at all in any part of this, and they are apt to conjure up instant rational explanations to make nonsense of it all. But none of it is for the brain; the brain cannot be expected to understand spirit. The way of death is not for intellectual analysis. A spiritual path moves us towards a state of inner wholeness, and as analysis involves the process of breaking down wholes into understandable parts, analysts will find nothing tangible, nothing solid to grasp. Intellectual analysis can yield nothing that makes sense, because the materiality on which science is based is not a participant. To the clever brain spiritual wholeness seems nonsense, because it is akin to non-existence. Only through the qualities of faith, patience, submission and sincerity can we participate in this process, and only through personal experience can we begin to understand it.

None can say how many years will pass for an individual whilst on the spiritual path. The process of purification, of renewing soul-contents, will probably never be complete; true perfection is unlikely to be found within the human condition. Our narrow path continues through what may seem the dull, dark interior of nature, passing major milestones along the way, reaching in turn the plant, the animal and then the human life forces, each imposing on the spiritual pilgrim its own subtle changes in outlook and attitude. As we finally approach the saintly level at the peak of humanity we shall understand the phrase 'God is love' as we begin to experience truly spiritual love for ourselves – the compassion which forms itself through the combination of all the separate passions; their positive outcome.

We shall discover that the personal souls which seemed to have died along the route did not in fact die, they did not disappear – they had kept their peace only because their passionate contents had been stilled. They will now be combining to form one truly human compassionate soul, a soul which is able to call upon the characteristics of each separate lower soul according to the needs of the moment, to meet any of life's situations. We may experience a return in some measure of the miraculous phenomena that we experienced when starting out along the path, but there is now nothing that could be used with ill intent. Finally our path emerges from the darkness of nature into the light, and not even physical death can check our progress into the world of spirit.

INDEX

Abraham 181
Acca Larentia 127
Achelous 53
aconite 74
Ahaz, sundial of 26
Adonis 111, 112, 141, 142
Aduramman 50
Aedon 88
Aganippe 59
Agatho-daemon 108, 113, 133
'age of reason' 153
Agrotera 150
Alban hills 40
alder king 151
Amalthea 54
Ammu 33
Anadyomene 47, 49
animal characteristics 169, 170
   soul 106, 169, 185
Anna Perenna 35
Annona 133
Aphrodite, Venus-Aphrodite 47, 49, 80, 81, 111, 112, 113, 134, 137, 141-179
Apis 142
Apollo 26-30, 48, 57, 59, 82, 87, 129, 130, 142
Apsu 42
Ares 128
Argus 35
Aristaeus 28, 98
Artemis, Diana-Artemis 26, 34, 49, 55, 75, 78, 80, 112, 118, 122, 129, 147, 150, 152, 160, 161, 180
Asaru 28
Ashtoreth 180
Asshur 26

Astarte 34, 79, 130, 180
astrology 38, 39
Asura 157
Atalanta 75, 137
Atargatis 75, 128, 180
Athene 82
Athtar 34
atonement 195
Attis 90, 112, 142, 160, 179
Aurora 24, 51, 82

Baal 130
   Moloch 74, 75
   -Zebub 90
Babylonia 26, 28, 33, 61-71
bacchanalia 108, 134
Bacchus-Dionysus 75, 76, 80, 108, 128, 134, 135, 140, 142, 149, 152, 179
balance, soul 175, 177-179, 180-182
bay laurel 57
Beelzebub 90
Bendis 34
Blake, William 97
bodhisattva 154, 156, 157
Bona Dea 108
bonsai 125, 126
Boreas 51
Borsippa 64, 70
Britomartis 34
Brizo 48
Buddha 154

cabiri 160
Caelestis 34
cakes, moon 36
Calliope 59

INDEX

caprotina 81
Castalia 57
castration, symbolic 180
Cerberus 15, 74, 138
Cedreatis 118
Celts 54, 55
Ceres 113, 129, 131, 139
Cernunnos 78, 158
Charles II 123
Chloe 131
Christian rebirth 104, 143, 180
Chronus 131
Circe 90
Clare, John 94
Clio 59
Cocytus 138
collective unconscious 57
compassion 145, 175, 176, 185
conservation 80
corn spirit 131
cornucopia 53, 132
Corylatus 160
creation, Babylonian 42
  Biblical 42
Cronos 131, 179
Crowley, Aleister 100
cruelty to animals 82
  to insects 91, 98
  to plants 106
Cupid 179
Cuthah 64
Cybele 75, 131, 142, 152
Cynthia 34, 50

Daedalus 85
Dagon 129, 130
Daniel 75
Daphne 57
Dea Dia 134
deer 78

delphinia 48
Delphia, Delphinius 49
Demeter 112, 113, 127, 129, 130, 133, 140
Deo 131
dharma, meaning of 90
Diana, Diana-Artemis 26, 34, 49, 55, 75, 78, 80, 112, 118, 122, 129, 147, 150, 152, 160, 161, 180
  shrine of 40, 41
Dianus 55
Dido 34, 57
diet, influence of 77
dietary laws 86, 87
dionysia 198, 134, 135
Dionysus, Bacchus-Dionysus 75, 76, 80, 108, 128, 134, 135, 140, 142, 149, 152, 179
dog 83
dolphin 48
Druids 136, 161
dryads 57, 123, 158
'dying god' 139, 141, 142, 143

eagle 87
Egeria 58, 59
Egypt, ancient 33
emasculation, symbolic 180
Endymion 147, 148
Enki 128
Enlil 51
entomology 91, 102
Epona 54, 82
Eos 24, 26
Erato 59
Erech 64
Erl-king 151
Eros 179
Erysichton 133

199

ESP 191
eternal youth 137
Eumolphos 107
Euphrates 62, 64, 65
Euploia 49
Euros 51
Euterpe 59
exercise, spiritual 190-197

faith, passion of 173, 185
Fatuus 150
Faunus 134, 150, 158
Favonius 51
festivals of Apollo 27
flies, influence of 90, 93, 94
Flora 51, 79
floralia 111
fontinalia 58
Fontus 58
fragmentation, perception of 92
Francis of Assisi 34
Frey 133
Freyr 50
Freyja 50
Frigg 132

Gaia 131
Galenia 49
Ganymede 179
gate of Ishtar 68, 70
Gatumdug 143
gazelle 79
Genesis, Book of 42, 52, 107, 177
gender of heavenly bodies 34
Gerda 50
Glanville, Lady 92, 93
Glaucous 46
Glyndwr, Owen 123
goat 80, 81
gnomes 153

gods, origin of 130
golden apples 137
Graham, W. S. 44
'grain mother' 131
Green Man 16, 17, 20, 103-105 157, 194
green woodpecker 109, 110
Grimm, brothers 45
gryphon 85, 86
Gymir 50

Hadad 50
Hades 112, 129, 138
Hafren 54
hamadryads 57, 123, 158
hare 79
harvest goddess 129
heaven, nature of 144, 145
Hebe 179
Hecate 34, 90, 98, 137, 147, 150
Heimdall 52
Heleia 56
Heliogabalus 26
Helios 26, 82, 110, 129
Hera 50, 88, 152
Hercules 29
Hermaphroditos 47, 49
Hermes 29, 52, 108, 128
Hertha 160
Hesperides 137
hippocampus 46
Hippomenes 75
hobgoblin 151
Holda 160
horse 30, 81, 82, 83, 84
Horus 87, 132, 143
hosts of heaven 25, 38
hugging a tree 115-126
human characteristics 165-169
  soul 167

INDEX

hunting 77-81, 150
  magic 78
Hyacinthus 112, 142

Icarus 85
ice-blink 50
Iduna 137
ignis fatuus 56
ikebana 113, 114, 115
images, superstition towards 25
Imkhursag 152
'imps of the forest' 151, 158
incense, original 191
Innini 141
insects, influence of 90-191
  in art 98
Io 37
Irene 110
Iris 52
Isaiah 26, 79, 84, 141
Ishtar 34, 64, 68, 70, 141
  gate 68, 70
Isis 53, 127, 132

Jack Frost 50
jack o' lantern 56
Janus 55, 104
Jeremiah 36, 60
Job 143, 155, 156
Jung, Carl Gustav 39, 56
Juno 34, 35, 88, 161
Jupiter 35, 38, 63, 70, 107, 108, 161
  symbolising Babylon 63

kelpie 44, 55
kindness, excessive 83
Kipling, Rudyard 83, 112
knockers, kobolds 153
Kronos 129, 130, 138

Lagash 64
Lake Nemi 40
leopard 75
Lethe 138
Leucothea 47
Liber, Libera 108
Libitina 108
life in retrospect 166
light of the material 169, 170, 171
  pollution 35
Lilith 51
Limnaia 55
lion 75, 76
locusts 98, 99
lord of the flies 90
love, misplaced 83
Lucifer 34, 167
Lud 54
Luna 34, 35
lunar year 33
lupercalia 152
Lupercus 152
Lycius 26
lynx 76

Ma 150
magic, natural 76, 77
mandala, world 174
Mani 34
Mars 38, 64, 128
marshes 56
material soul 165, 168
materiality, definition of 164-165
Marduk 62-71
  sacred path of 62, 66
meditation 72
  on the moon 37
Melainis 49
Melicertes 46
Melissa 54, 98

201

Melkart 46
Melpomene 59
Mercury 38, 64, 70, 128
Merlin 184
Minerva 88, 110
Minotaur 74
mirror of Diana 40
mistletoe 135, 136
Mithras 26, 152
Mnemosyne 59
moon, attributes of 32-37
   feast 35
   goddesses 34, 35
   meditating on 37
Moses 25, 26, 86, 87, 181
Moslem calendar 33
Muchia 49
Myrrha 112
Myrtea 112

Nabopolassar 69, 70
Nabu, Nebu 64, 70
Nannar 33
narcotics 113
nature, integrity of 92
Nebuchadnezzar 62-71
Neptune 39, 46, 140
Nergal 64, 75, 76
Nertha 133
Nerthus 160
Nereus 46
Ninindug 143
Ninkarrak 143
Nintud 152
Ninurta 64, 143
Niobe 59
Niordhir 50
Nisroch 26
Noah 52, 107
Noctiluca 35

Notus 51
Nusku 33
nymphs 57-59

Oannes 46
Oceanus 46, 138
Odin, Woden 88, 127
olives 110
omens 87, 88
opalia 133
Ops 133
Orion 38
Osiris 107, 128, 132, 142

Palaemon 46
Pallas Athene 110, 127
Pan 57, 108, 128, 134, 150, 151,
   152, 158
Pandemos 81
paniskoi 151
Panoptes 26
paradise, the nature of 166
passions, the nature of 171
Periphlegethon 138
pentagram 81
Persephone 90, 108, 112, 129,
   131, 138, 139, 140, 141
Phaeton 26
Phoebe 34
Phoebus 26
Picus 109, 110, 158
planets personalised 38
plant characteristics 14, 158, 159
   essence 108
   kingdom, people aligned with
     105
   paradise 113
   people 105, 103
   soul 106
plants sacred to Apollo 30

INDEX

Pliny 124
Pluto 39, 90, 129, 137, 138
Plutus 137
Polyhymnia 59
Pomona 110
porpoises 48
Portunus 46, 47
Poseidon 46, 140
prayer, reality of 190, 191
Priapus 98, 107, 128, 134
Proserpina 129, 131, 138, 139, 140
Proteus 46
Puck 151
purgatory 145
pyanepsia 129
Python 28

queen of heaven 50
rainbow 52, 53
Ray, John 93
reincarnation 143, 144
religious decline 169-171
Revelation, biblical 52, 145
Rhea 75, 107, 127, 152
Rhiannon 54, 55, 82
rhythm of life 93
Rimmon, Ramman 50
rising sun 31, 32
Robin Goodfellow 151
roc 16, 86
Rosmerta 132
Rumina, Ruminus 109

Sabazius 143
Sabrina, Sabre 54
sacred path of Marduk 62-71
  river 62
sacrifice, magical 100
SAD 28
Samsu 33

Satan, realm of 17, 20, 34, 105, 194
Saturn, Saturnus 38, 64, 129, 130, 133
saturnalia 131, 133
satyrs 79, 134
scarabs, Egyptian 100
sea, emotional effect of 44, 45
Selene 26, 34, 147, 150, 152
Semes 33, 34
serpent, realm of the 20, 85
Shakespeare, William 45, 90
shamanic forces 73
Shamash 26, 34, 64
Shantideva 156, 157
Silenus 108
Silvanus 158
Sin, the moon god 33
smells, ethereal 81, 191
Sol as a goddess 34
soul, animal 106, 169, 185
  brothers and sisters 184
  human 167
  material 165, 168
  plant 106
  receptive 178
souls, personal 193
Sozon 46
spiritualism 190
stone circles 132
Styx 138
submission 72
Subud 183
Summanus 33
Sumohadiwidjojo, Muhammad Subuh 190
sun as a destiny 30
  attributes of 27-32
sundial of Ahaz 26
Sutherland, Graham 98
Svetasvatara upanishad 61

synchronicity 39
Syrinx 57

tamarisk 66
Tammuz 53, 141
Tartarus 138
Terpsichore 59
Thalia 59
thalusia 130
thanksgiving 132
Thor 50, 123
Thoth 33
Tiamat 42
Tigris 63
trance state 73, 190
trees, influence of 115-126
triad, universal 127
Triptolemus 142
Triton 46
trolls 153

upanishads 30, 61, 143
Ur 34
Urania 59
Uranus 39, 179

Varley, John 97
vegetation, deities of 127-143

Venus, Venus-Aphrodite 38, 47, 49, 64, 70, 80, 81, 111, 112, 113, 134, 137, 141, 179
Vertumnos 110, 111
vibrations of nature 91
  of the inner self 159, 163, 181, 183, 189
vinalia 108
voodoo 73

Wadd 33
wanderlust 14
water in creation 41
  symbolising emotions 40-60
  symbolising spirit 61-71
waterspout 44
wedding ceremonies 29
wendigo 148
'wild wanderer' 152
will o' the wisp 56
Woden, Odin 88, 127
Wordsworth, William 53
world mandala 174

Zagros mountains 68
Zephyrus 51, 112, 142
Zeus 59, 88, 148, 179
Zu 42

www.ingramcontent.com/pod-product-compliance
Lightning Source LLC
Chambersburg PA
CBHW060513090426
42735CB00011B/2209